HOW TO LOVE THE WORLD
WITHOUT FALLING FOR IT

TOO
CHRISTIAN
TOO
PAGAN

DICK STAUB

ZondervanPublishingHouse
Grand Rapids, Michigan

A Division of HarperCollins*Publishers*

Library of Congress Cataloging-in-Publication Data

Staub, Dick, 1948–
    Too Christian, too pagan: how to love the world without falling for it
/ Dick Staub.
      p.   cm.
    Includes bibliographical references.
    ISBN: 0-310-23315-1
    1. Christian life.   I. Title.
    BV4501.2.S7365   2000
    248.4–dc21   00-033381

This edition is printed on acid-free paper.

Interior design by Melissa Elenbaas
Printed in the United States of America

01 02 03 04 05 /❖ DC/ 10 9 8 7 6 5 4 3 2

For Keith Green, Bob Briner,
Bill Lane, and Rich Mullins
Each knew what it meant to be perceived
as too Christian and too pagan
and inspired me and so many others
to take Jesus into our world

CONTENTS

■ ACKNOWLEDGMENTS

S O MANY PEOPLE HAVE BUMPED THE TRAJECTORY OF MY LIFE'S direction, and while all of them may not agree with my ideas or where I am on the journey, they have been kind enough to acknowledge me. So I return the favor to a few, with apologies to countless others whom I've forgotten to mention.

My grandfather Walter and grandmother Cora Staub were exemplary, steady influences toward knowing God by following Jesus. My mother, Esther, father, Dick Sr., sisters, Becky and Ruthy, and mother-in-law, Pat, while often concerned about my coloring outside the lines, kept providing me with fresh crayons.

Don Kenyon's course on Romans helped me realize that Jesus is universal and for all, even though the religion named after him often degenerates into a narrow, cloistered, unappealing subculture. When Bill Lane took the gospel to Mardi Gras or did theological analysis of Ingmar Bergman films from the original Swedish, I could hear the apostle Paul at Mars Hill more clearly. The same thing happened when Earl Palmer saw the original *Star Wars* on Saturday and used it as a framework for the next day's sermon. David Scholer pushed me to understand gospel text in light of a first-century cultural context. He also introduced me to Chaim Potok, who helped me see my own Christian subculture through the eyes of a young Hasidic Jew struggling with his subculture. Bishop Steven Neill helped me craft approaches for dialogue with Islam, and Martin Marty helped me toward a broader dialogue within Christianity.

Art Miller and Ralph Mattson helped me understand the nature of personal God-given giftedness and provided theological and ideological justification for my irrepressible urges toward the new, novel, and different.

Dave Petersen and Marty O'Donnell met with me for breakfast every week while I was writing this book, then stopped meeting with me just because I moved two thousand miles away.

Somehow, Sealy and Tom convinced Scott and Stan to offer me a contract for this book. Then they convinced Lyn and Lori to edit it and Cindy to do a cover, and before any responsible adults could intervene it got published, and the marketing department had to figure out how to sell it. They were successful enough to get you to buy it, and I'll thank you in advance because if everything goes according to plan, you will actually read it.

My wife, Kathy, and kids—Joshua, Jessica, Heidi, and Molly—keep me tethered to the ground when the big ideas and hot air threaten to lift my head from my body. They laugh, love, forgive, challenge, and reinvigorate me so my spirit and mind are sustained and renewed each day.

Most of all, every good and perfect gift comes from above. Thank you, God.

■ PREFACE

The inexhaustible urge towards self-expression makes it nearly a sure thing that there will always be writers around. The dicier question is whether there will be readers. Not just readers of the sports pages and the jumble of self-help best-sellers and the consultant's confessions, no, but passionate readers who ignore the phone and the TV for a few hours to engage a book whose "difficulty" is that it fails to soothe the ego or flatter a limited intelligence; the reader who honestly believes that the best and deepest of what we are is on the shelf, and that to read across the shelf changes the self, changes you.

DAVID REMNICK,
THE NEW YORKER

IN JAPAN THEY DON'T think people should write books until they are fifty. The theory is you don't really have anything worth saying until then. Or maybe you have something to say, but you haven't lived it long enough to prove it is true. I love those Japanese, and I made their deadline by a year.

This book is about my experiences following Jesus into the world. My career has taken me to different settings: to over forty countries; to a large corporate environment; to a few entrepreneurial ventures; to a religious nonprofit organization; and to broadcasting, both general market talk radio and Christian-formatted talk radio. In each of these settings I've tried to be an effective presence for the gospel and discovered it is not an easy thing to do.

My initial forays into the world were a lot like the late John Denver's fatal flight in an experimental aircraft. We now know that Denver carried insufficient fuel (his first fuel tank ran dry after only sixteen minutes in flight) and had received inadequate training (only a ten-minute checkout flight), and that is why he plummeted to his death.

My early years as a Christian in the world were similarly lacking in preparation and resources and, but for the grace of God, might have also resulted in disaster. However, though I've made a lot of mistakes, I avoided the fatal ones. So you hold in your hands a book containing some of my observations after over thirty-five years of intentionally trying to make a difference in my corner of the world.

There are twenty-five relatively short chapters in this book, the idea being you can read one a day, even skip a few days, and still work through in less than a month what has taken me over thirty-five years to learn. As my eight-year-old daughter, Molly, would say, "I guess Daddy was in the slow group!"

I hope as a fellow sojourner you will find trustworthy pointers as you blaze a trail on the road less traveled, taking Jesus into your world whatever and wherever that world may be.

TOO CHRISTIAN, TOO PAGAN

I
IN AN AGE OF UNPARALLELED MATERIAL prosperity, our world is unraveling. As a talk show host I observed this by reading five newspapers and skimming nine hundred select articles daily, as well as perusing an average of twenty review copies of new books each week. Emerging from this rubble of information is a portrait of the modern world as "an uncomfortable, unfulfilling place to live" as a 1995 *Time* magazine cover story titled "Twentieth Century Blues" once concluded. The rapid spread of societal decay

into our everyday lives seems indisputable, inevitable, and even more pervasive now that we're in the twenty-first century.

For followers of Jesus, this volatile world poses a grave threat. When living counter to culture, Christians are despised and hated by the world. When conforming to culture, Christians risk succumbing to the seductive desires of the flesh, the lust of the eyes, and the pride of riches (see 1 John 2:16). Most of us know people who jettisoned their faith for the momentary pleasures of this age, and all of us experience and sometimes give in to the kinds of temptations that, if unchecked, lead to the contamination of our spirit.

Today, Christian responses to the world include de facto *withdrawal* into a protective cocoon, *combat* in the culture war, or a widespread, chameleonlike *conformity*. Our instincts for personal spiritual survival warn us to stay clear of this alternatingly inhospitable and enticing place. Yet ironically, this soul-threatening society also offers our greatest opportunity for influence, because an unraveling society produces a spiritually restless people needing Jesus' transforming good news.

THE SPIRITUALITY CRAZE

And so it is that in today's uncertain and anxious hour, "spirituality," once a taboo subject, is now mainstreamed, an acceptable topic for everyday conversation. "The spiritual" permeates film, music, and best-selling books. In her book *God-Talk in America, Publisher Weekly's* former religion editor Phyllis Tickle concludes, "More theology is conveyed in, and probably retained from one hour of popular television, than from all the sermons that are also delivered on any given weekend in America's synagogues, churches, and mosques."

On television in a three-week span Larry King interviewed the Dalai Lama, Benny Hinn, and Billy Graham. On the fortieth anniversary celebration of King's broadcasting career, Bryant Gumble asked, "Larry, if you could interview God, what would your first question be?" King responded quickly, "I'd ask God—do you have a son?"

Today's spiritual journey is increasingly carried on outside organized religion. This is especially true for the next generation. A survey from the University of Chicago's National Opinion Research Center reveals that in 1998, among eighteen- to twenty-two-year-olds, only 16 percent had any contact with organized religion. Yet they have a higher interest in spiritual issues than the same generation twenty years earlier, with 82 percent of them asking questions about life after death compared to only 69 percent in 1978. They are more likely to seek answers to their questions in a Barnes and Noble bookstore, or in discussions about recently released movies or music, than they are in a church. Because today's spiritual conversation has moved outside the church and into everyday life, it is more essential than ever that you and I engage people where they are in the rough and tumble world.

Too Christian, Too Pagan

This poses a problem. Most of us want to make a positive difference in our circle of influence, yet we feel woefully inadequate to take Jesus into our world. There are two equal and opposite reasons for this. In my observation most Christians are either too Christian or too pagan.* The Christians who are "too Christian" are very comfortable within the Christian subculture but are ill at ease when in the world. On the other hand, Christians who are too pagan are at ease with the world but fail to integrate their faith into their everyday life.*

Taking Jesus into our world requires fully engaging both our faith and the world, yet few of us have learned to live a

---

* While paganism is a religion, at one time it was common to classify people as either Christians or pagans. (In other eras, *paganism* has been used to mean anyone who isn't a Christian, Muslim, or Jew.) I'm using the word *pagan* in the archaic and colloquial sense. My apologies for any offense caused to people who practice paganism or those of other religions who prefer not to be classified as pagans. None intended.

fully integrated life of faith in the world. Paradoxically, in my experience those who wholeheartedly embark on this path will end up seeming both too Christian for their pagan friends and too pagan for their Christian friends.

This was certainly true for Jesus. Read the gospels and you'll see how Jesus' nonconformity in religious *and* pagan culture made him somewhat alien to both. The religious were suspicious because Jesus partied with pagans—drunkards, prostitutes, and tax collectors, to name a few. The pagans loved Jesus' company, but eventually were uncomfortable when he challenged them to make radical changes in their personal lives. The woman caught in the act of adultery was forgiven, but was also told to go and sin no more. Zacchaeus, the tax collector, ended up repaying everyone he had defrauded and giving half his wealth to the poor.

Because Jesus was determined to please God instead of humans, he was a nonconformist. In fact, Jesus was a winsome, compelling character precisely because God—not the culture nor the religious subculture—set his daily agenda. He clearly marched to the beat of a different drummer.

Following Jesus today requires you to practice that same single-minded nonconformity. And it will produce the same effect in your life that it did with Jesus. If you truly follow Jesus, in addition to enjoying a most excellent adventure, you will likely end up seeming too Christian for many of your pagan friends and too pagan for many of your Christian friends. When you truly follow Jesus, you'll spend considerable time and energy in the world like he did, and as a result, many of your religious friends will think you're too irreligious. On the other hand, many of your irreligious friends will find it odd that you are so focused on the spiritual. Thus, you end up seeming both too Christian and too pagan.

One friend agreed with me and then said, "It sounds like a lose-lose! Why would anybody want to end up out of sync with both their pagan and their Christian friends?" This book will try to provide a compelling answer to that question. In addition, it will show you how you can be more effective in taking Jesus into your world.

For some, this book will improve spiritual literacy, and for others, it will improve cultural literacy. In both cases, the hoped-for result is progress toward becoming disciples literate in both faith and culture, disciples experiencing the joy of becoming a complete person and a confident, compelling presence for Jesus.

CHAPTER 2

YIELD TO GOD'S GOVERNANCE

ONE SUMMER DAY IN THE SIXTIES, MY brother-in-law and I were racing down the highway with the top down in my powder blue MGB convertible. A yield sign warned me of traffic merging on the right. The vehicle barreling into my lane was an eighteen-wheeler, but in my youthful exuberance I yelled out at the top of my lungs, "Back-off, buddy!" For some reason the trucker did not feel compelled to comply with my request and I lost the mismatch, but Phil and I still chuckle at how this story illustrates my full-speed-ahead personality.

The need to yield to God, however, is no laughing matter. The single most common reason we live unintegrated lives is that we believe our little MGB and God's eighteen-wheeler can share the same space. Our behavior often suggests that when one of us must yield, we think that God should just back off. This will never work. Soren Kierkegaard said, "Purity of heart is to will one thing," and as we've already pointed out, Jesus was effective in the world because of his single-minded devotion to God's will. So the first step in becoming effective for Jesus in the world is to yield governance of your life to God.

What I learned on the highway in my MGB I began learning in my spiritual life during the first semester of college. Like many other college students I had—to borrow a phrase from the parable of the Prodigal Son—"wasted my life in riotous living." I was enjoying new friends, a new city (San Francisco), a lot of parties, and an occasional class—not a formula for academic success. On the bus ride home to Spokane for Christmas break, I commiserated with my life-long friend Jimmie about the meaninglessness of life and our lives in particular.

More was expected of us. Our parents had graduated from college together. From his youth, Jimmie's mother dutifully conducted a private summer school to assure the academic success of her children. My father earned an advanced degree while raising a family and pastoring a growing church. I was a third-generation preacher's kid with all the weight of expectations and future glories resting on my stupefied head. We knew we were headed down the wrong path, so Jimmie and I covenanted to spend the holiday season considering our wicked ways, cleaning the slate, and seeking dramatically fresh, new directions.

Alas, how destinies take unique and often unexpected twists and turns. During that very Christmas break, Jimmie was involuntarily relieved of his academic calling, receiving a higher calling in the form of a draft notice, personally inviting him to serve our beloved country with a tour of duty in Viet Nam. (Lest you wonder, he survived, and today is a pastor, undoubtedly not eager to have the details of his freshman year revealed on these pages.) I, on the other hand, received notice from a different higher power and, in a way, that also radically changed the course of my life.

A MOMENT THAT CHANGED MY LIFE

It was a snowy Spokane day, a great day for staying in, sitting by the warmth of a poorly tended fire, and contemplating one's uncertain fate. My parents, ever dutiful pastor and wife, felt compelled to visit a hospitalized parishioner and asked me to keep an eye on my brother Timmy.

Timmy was stricken with cerebral palsy from birth, unable to walk or talk. Though only ten when Timmy was born, I was already somewhat suspicious and distanced from this "God thing" which so captivated my family. By disposition I was a free spirit and felt boxed in by the quasi-legalistic tradition in which I was being raised. Timmy's severe brain damage at birth compounded my discontent with God.

I could not understand how a loving God would allow such devastation. It made no sense that my devout, sacrificial parents would receive such an unjust reward. I was asking the kinds of questions humans have asked throughout history, unaware of theirs, believing mine to be original, somehow knowing intuitively that my own answers would lead either to the birth of an authentic, robust faith or to faith's aborted, embittered death. In this way, though mute, Timmy spoke volumes to me and shaped my spiritual trajectory. Whatever possibility, however remote given my nature, that mine would be a simple, naïve embracing of faith, died at my brother's birth. God and I would do a rigorous, contentious business or none at all.

So, at the age of ten, my ship of personal faith encountered blustery, tempestuous winds. During my late teens, I began negotiating something of a truce with God, and through a long series of events, by the snowy day during that winter break from college, I was entering faith's safe harbor and dropping anchor. My faith was still tentative, and I was not contemplating a venture into the open seas. As is so often the case, God had other plans.

On that wintry day, earnest in my desire to remedy my waywardness, I was reading my Bible while Tim crawled aimlessly on the floor.

You hear about God speaking audibly to people, you hear stories of people finding a random Bible verse that is so pointedly applicable it is as if God spoke directly to them. This is not what happened that day. Rather, my message came through the groan of my spastic brother and his gnarled hand landing on a verse of Scripture from Paul's epistle to the Romans.

Timmy cannot talk. He laughs, he grunts, he makes his wishes and feelings known through inarticulate sounds interpretable only after years of practice and aided by an active imagination. But something different happened that day. It never happened before and hasn't happened since. As I read the Bible, Timmy crawled stealthily toward me, rose to his knees, and with his vicelike grip, grabbed both my arms, looked me in the face, and tried to say the word *brother*. His guttural dynamic equivalent exploded with full force and spittle in my face. BRUV!

A sweeter sound I will not hear in this life.

One bent and twisted hand fell off my arm and straight onto the Bible open on my lap. Romans 12:1: "I urge you ... in view of God's mercy, to offer your bodies as living sacrifices, holy and pleasing to God—this is your spiritual act of worship."

Bodies. My brother's body twisted with nerves and muscles intermittently misfiring, and disconnected from its neurological control central—and mine, healthy, strong, and certain. Which, I wondered, is most pleasing to God? Is it the son doing the best he can within the constraints of his fated mortal coil, or is it the son who squanders, in pointless distractions and inanities, his abilities to walk, talk, and form relationships between ideas and with people?

ONE KINGDOM, ONLY ONE KING

Profound epiphanies are rare. Call it a defining moment. Call it God's wide mercy beckoning me off a path leading to a self-absorbed, gray, existential funk, onto one bursting with passion.

Clarity.

On this wintry day, I reached a fork in the road and knew I must choose one or the other. My memory banks involuntarily recalled words from my upbringing, now effortlessly and instantly retrieved: "No man can serve two masters," "Seek first the kingdom of God," "You are not your own, you've been bought with a price, therefore glorify God in your body."

Clarity.

One road leads to God's kingdom, but requires the coronation of God because in God's kingdom there can be only one King. I vaguely recalled Dutch theologian Abraham Kuyper's phrase, "There is not one square inch of the entire creation about which Jesus Christ does not cry out, 'This is mine! This belongs to me.'"

I, Dick Staub, a befuddled, lowly freshman, was engaged in a seismic paradigm shift that would alter the course of my entire life. In my own limited way, I understood intuitively that the decision regarding which road I would take and who would govern me on that road was the fundamental, core, rock-bottom issue every human being faces when encountering God.

Jesus warned prospective disciples to take this decision seriously. His was a radical call to self-denial, sacrifice, the daily taking up of a cross, a willingness to follow wherever he might lead. As Dallas Willard once said to me, Jesus never called anyone to be a Christian, he only called people to be a disciple. The choice is clear: Jesus wants everything in our life, or nothing at all.

The King James Version emphasizes that making God central in life is *reasonable* because God has been so merciful (Romans 12:1). Presenting ourselves to God and living life for God is our highest, deepest act of worship. Living this way requires a renewing of your mind, a transformation of the way you think, from simple conformity to the way the world thinks, to nonconformity (Romans 12:2).

Today, yielding governance of your life to God is more radical and countercultural than ever because the late twentieth century has been characterized by a total devotion to self and the twenty-first seems to be more of the same. We have collectively embraced the mantra expressed in Frank Sinatra's signature song, "I did it my way." There is even a magazine called *Self.* At the root of today's secularist society is the axiom, "Man is the measure of all things." This glorification of self is so pervasive it can even extend to our religious choices. Who can forget in *Habits of the Heart* sociologist Robert Bellah's interview with Sheila, who said she had discovered a new religion, "Sheila-ism!"

The problem, of course, is that axiomatic to the Judeo-Christian tradition is God as the measure of all things. This is why the proper perspective on oneself is the first step toward presenting our body to God as a living sacrifice. Paul said, "[Do] not think of yourself more highly than you ought to think, but ... think with sober judgment" (Romans 12:3). One of my favorite posters says simply, "There is a God. You are not Him."

THE ROAD LESS TRAVELED

Having covenanted to spend the holiday season considering my wicked ways, cleaning the slate, and seeking dramatically fresh, new directions, I was getting something more personal, specific, and radical than I had hoped for. This literally was the fork in the road. This was the moment that would shape the balance of my life.

Robert Frost wrote of such a fork in the road: "Two roads diverged in a yellow wood, and I—I took the one less traveled by. And that has made all the difference." That wintry day I decided to follow the road less traveled, waving the white flag, surrendering, submitting to the new, true, worthy King of my life. The explorer in me felt the rush of enthusiasm for forging into the unknown under new management.

Since that day I have learned it is true, as has so often been said, that "the problem with living sacrifices is they can crawl off the altar!" My one-time life-altering decision allowing God to govern my life is one I reconfirm every day. Without his governance it is easy to slip into a life that is either too pagan or too Christian. But my daily decision to yield governance of my life to God keeps me from becoming too pagan when in the world, and keeps me going into the world when I feel like hanging out with the saints all the time.

I'll add a comment here for those of you who are married. Marriage is the union of two people who become one. As a married person your individual decision to yield to God's governance is either enhanced or encumbered by the commitment of your spouse. God's blessing and promise to Abraham could only be fulfilled with Sarah's cooperation. Our decisions to move to Chicago in 1991 and back to Seattle in 1999 required my wife and me to discern God's will together. Because I am so highly individualistic and Kathy is collaborative, she has taught me a lot about mutuality. Whatever we accomplish for the kingdom of God will be a testimony to two people who have decided to yield to God's sovereignty. Choosing the road less traveled *together* involves a mutual yielding to God and requires an attentiveness to your spouse's relationship with God, nurturing a prayer life together, and enjoying the help God has provided in bringing two very different people together as one.

In *Power Through Prayer*, E. M. Bounds said, "God is ready to assume full responsibility for the life that is fully yielded to Him." If you have never yielded your life to God, or you have gotten in the habit of taking back the reins, I pray that you will ask God to govern your life right this moment. It is in continuous yielding to the governance of God that you can discover the single-mindedness that makes it possible to live an engaging, fully integrated life.

LEAVE YOUR COMFORT ZONE

ONCE YOU HAVE YIELDED THE GOVernance of your life to God and committed yourself to following Jesus, I can guarantee that Jesus will begin to call you outside your comfort zone and into new territory. In *God in the Dock*, C. S. Lewis put it this way, "I didn't go to religion to make me happy. I always knew a bottle of port would do that. If you want a religion to make you feel really comfortable, I certainly wouldn't recommend Christianity." The disciples discovered this to be true all the way from their first encounter with Jesus right through to the end. His first words were "follow me." His parting words were "go into the world." Every step along the way Jesus told his followers to leave everything they knew, their jobs, their homes, their hometowns—always for unknown destinies. His benefit package was not insignificant. He said he would never leave them or forsake them. He said if they sought his kingdom first, he would provide for their every need.

Now here is the truly exciting news. Nothing has changed. As spiritual descendants of Jesus' disciples, we are commanded to go into the world just as they were. Jesus wants us in the world to love, bless, and transform the world through our presence and witness for the gospel. There are really only two troublesome elements in Jesus' commandment to "go into the world." First, there's the part about *going*, and second, the part about going *into the world.* Other than that, it seems pretty doable!

STAYING IS EASIER THAN GOING

This is all intensely fresh stuff for me. I'm writing this in a McDonald's in Naperville, Illinois. Our realtor evicted me from my house about an hour ago for entirely understandable reasons. Today our house was put up for sale, and by noon we'd received multiple offers. Realtor Don thought if the gregarious "yours truly" stayed in the house I'd mess up the deal, so he begged Kathy to "get that husband of yours" out of the house. So here I sit.

It is a very emotional day, and I'll tell you why. Staying is easier than going. We've lived here for eight years and have come to love this place. We're part of a wonderful church where we've been befriended by some of the finest people we know. Our home backs on to a forest preserve complete with prairie grass, bluebird boxes, trails, and a river meandering through old oak trees. We are situated in the world's nicest neighborhood in a home decorated just the way we like it and conveniently located near all the things we like—a neighborhood pool and tennis courts, a thirty-plex movie theater with stadium-style seating, the best restaurants in the Chicago suburbs, and shopping galore. Plus, we're within an easy drive or train ride to Chicago, a world-class city in every regard.

Never mind that we experienced this same rush of emotions when we left Seattle eight years ago, and never mind that we're moving back to Seattle where we have every reason to believe God will provide more than we ask. Never mind that most of our relatives live in the Northwest. Never mind that for six of our eight years here I longed for the Northwest and couldn't wait to move back. Now that we can "go home," we all feel the strongest possible urges to stay put. It's just a fact of life—staying is easier than going.

When it comes to following Jesus, there is just one problem with this human desire for the status quo. Jesus is always on the move, and he wants us to follow him. Granted, in his life on earth he covered a relatively confined patch of earth. One New Testament scholar calls him a simple Mediterranean peasant, and another refers to his life as rather provincial. Visit Israel and you'll see how small the territory he covered was. Take comfort in this because it means his call to "go" doesn't always require traveling great geographic distances.

In our case, we believe Jesus has asked us to physically relocate 2,200 miles away. Sometimes Jesus required that kind of relocation in the first century too. The first Christians heard his words to go to Jerusalem, Judea, and the uttermost parts of the earth, and so they obeyed and went to all those places. Listen to the roster of cities where the disciples died and you see their mobility: Matthew (Ethiopia), Mark (Alexandria, Egypt), Luke (Greece), John (Ephesus via Rome), Peter (Rome), Thomas (East Indies), and Simeon (Persia).

But even if we were to stay in Naperville, this "going" business would still apply. Sometimes Jesus told people specifically to stay put and be a witness where they were. After being healed, some new disciples wanted to climb on the gospel bus and hit the road with the traveling Savior. Jesus told many of them to stay in their own villages. He wanted everybody to hear the good news, one person at a time, and he figured leaving a few witnesses was the best way to accomplish this objective. You've heard of management by wandering around. Jesus was into "sharing the gospel by wandering around."

Now this is the second truly challenging thing about Jesus. While we like to stay in the comfort of our home and church, *Jesus tells us to go into the world.* In his view, church and home are havens for rest and recuperation, but they are supposed to be safety nets, not hammocks! He sends us into the world, and needless to say, the world can be a dangerous place.

I told you *where* the first disciples died, but not *how.* As Paul Harvey says, "Here's the rest of the story." While initially the church found favor with all in Jerusalem (Acts 2:47), it wasn't long before it was spoken against everywhere (Acts 28:22). This growing animosity toward the early Christians exacted a great price from Jesus' followers.

Stephen was martyred outside Jerusalem, Matthew in Ethiopia. Mark was dragged to his death through the streets of Alexandria. Luke was hanged from an olive tree in Greece. John survived a boiling pot of water at Rome, then died a natural death in Ephesus. Peter was crucified in Rome. James the Great was beheaded in Jerusalem. James the Less was thrown from the roof of the Temple and then beaten to death with a club. Philip was hanged against a pillar at Hierapolis in Phrygia. Thomas was stuck with a spear in the East Indies; Bartholomew was killed by having his skin ripped off while still alive. Jude was shot to death with arrows, Simeon crucified in Persia, and Paul had his head cut off in Rome by Nero. These are not exactly the kind of stories you want to put in the recruiting brochure for a new organization.

Nevertheless people keep signing up. The fate of those early Christian martyrs is shared by their spiritual descendants today. On my trips to China, I've heard numerous firsthand reports from house-church members who have been imprisoned and tortured for their faith, and these stories of modern-day martyrs can be heard in countries throughout the world. While uncommon in the United States, it can happen here as well.

In 1999 we were all shocked by the slaughter of twelve students and one teacher at Columbine High School in Littleton, Colorado. A widely reported and confirmed story tells of one student's final moments at Columbine.

A frightened girl lying on the cafeteria floor was asked by one of the gunmen if she believed in God. Knowing full well the safe answer, she followed her convictions and answered honestly. "There is a God," she said quietly, "and you need to follow along God's path." The gunman looked down at her. "There is no God," he said, and he shot her in the head.

Just the day before, Cassie Bernall, one of the victims, had written a poem and entered it in her diary.

Now I have given up on everything else
I have found it to be the only way
To really know Christ and to experience
The mighty power that brought
Him back to life again, and to find
Out what it means to suffer and to
Die with him. So, whatever it takes
I will be one who lives in the fresh
Newness of life of those who are
Alive from the dead.

Throughout the centuries relatively few Christians have been martyred for Jesus. We may die of embarrassment, but few of us will face the literal loss of life for our faith. However, it is clear that staying is easier than going out into the world. But then, Jesus never promised us we could stay in our comfort zone. Jesus calls us to go into the world. This is scary when we think about the hostile world we are entering, but God loved the world enough to send his own Son into the world, and he calls us to follow in his footsteps.

CHAPTER 4

■ LOVE THE WORLD

THE CHRISTIAN WHO IS TOO CHRIStian doesn't love the world enough to enter fully into it, and the Christian who is too pagan doesn't love Jesus enough to make a difference while there. Yet as disciples we are supposed to live out our calling in the world because Jesus commanded us to go into the world as a loving and transforming presence. Those who are too Christian often argue that they avoid the world because God tells us not to love the world or the things of the world. So how do we both love and not love the world at the same time? I begin with a story of a day in the life of a talk show host.

The phone lines were jammed, and I owed it all to Ann Landers. Her column that morning told the story of a young man named Bob who was about to be married. Bob was asking if he should un-invite his father Jim's "significant other" from the wedding ceremony. Fourteen years earlier Jim announced that he was gay and left Bob's mother. Jim now lived with Greg, a man who by all accounts was a kind and thoughtful person. Bob struggled with his father's decision. While he didn't approve of his father's choice, Bob had come to accept him. On occasion Bob and his fiancée Carol socialized with Jim and Greg.

When Carol's parents heard about this gay union, they were extremely upset and demanded that Greg not attend the wedding. When Greg learned of the situation he said he understood and told Bob he would voluntarily withdraw from the event. But Bob's dad was deeply offended and asked his son to reconsider. You be the judge. What would you do in this situation?

The calls came fast and were intense. "The bride's parents are being ridiculous. If Bob and his fiancée let her parents make this decision, they'll never stop interfering in this marriage." "Bob's dad is just reaping the benefits of his sinful act. First he leaves his wife, and then he takes up with a man. He should get over his hurt and accept the consequences of his own actions." "I think what Greg is doing is admirable—this couple should accept his peacemaking offer as a wonderful gift."

Then Pete from Long Beach called. "Not only should they tell Greg not to attend, they should make sure only born-again Christians attend their wedding."

"And why is that?" I asked.

"Marriage is a Christian ceremony, a sacrament, and we shouldn't pollute it with the presence of unbelievers."

"Sounds like a pretty radical position to me!"

"That's your problem, Dick, you don't understand the importance of separation from the world."

"Really! Tell me more."

"The Bible makes it clear. We are to have no fellowship with darkness. Friendship with the world is enmity with God. Dick, if you believe this, why do you do movie reviews every Thursday on your show?"

"And what do movie reviews have to do with it?"

"We're not supposed to love the world or the things of the world. The world is polluted with sin, and God is going to destroy it anyway! Movies are of the world! We shouldn't waste our time talking about them, and Christians certainly shouldn't be watching them."

"Pete, just so I'm sure I understand you, would you invite movie-going Christians to your wedding, or are they on the non-invite list with all the gays and non-Christians?"

"A real Christian wouldn't go to the movies, but you know what, Dick? You're a jerk, and I don't want to waste any more time putting my pearls in front of swine like you." *Click.* Pete hung up.

I'm in talk-show heaven because the phone lines are really cooking now. But I'm also concerned about Pete and what he said.

SHOULD WE LOVE THE WORLD?

How did Pete reach the conclusion that only "born-again Christians" should attend a Christian wedding? And how did he conclude that real Christians don't go to movies? And what does the destruction of the world have to do with it?

In his own way Pete was articulating ideas held in various forms and degrees of intensity among some Christians today. Their logic unfolds like this. The planet earth is a wicked place destined for destruction. Prior to salvation, individuals are wicked. After salvation Christians aspire to be holy, which requires them to separate from the world and every-thing in it. The only reason to stay in this world is to announce God's holy wrath and to "save as many sinners as we can." Jesus will return soon, and this wretched planet and all its pathetic inhabitants will be destroyed. The conclusion? Our only value as humans is our association with God, other-wise we are wretches. To summarize: God is good, the world is bad, Christians are good, and everybody else is bad.

Pete is basing his view on some biblical references that I believe he misinterprets and misapplies. "Do not love the world or the things in the world. . . . For all that is in the world . . . comes not from the Father but from the world" (1 John 2:15–16). "Do you not know that friendship with the world is enmity with God?" (James 4:4).

Have you ever noticed this apparent schizophrenia about God's relationship to the world and our own calling in it? How can God love the world (John 3:16) and command us to love even our enemies, yet at the same time command us to "not love the world or the things in the world" (1 John 2:15)? How can God send his Son into the world, command us to go into the world, yet at the same time command us to "be separate" and to "come out from" unbelievers (2 Co-rinthians 6:17)?

So which is it? Does God love the world? Should we? Is the world completely evil and to be avoided, or may we enjoy the world? Answering correctly requires understanding the vari-ety of ways the word *world* is used in the biblical record. It also requires understanding the implications of God as both Creator and Savior.

THE MEANING OF *WORLD*

First, let's look at the issue of language. Ancient languages offered a variety of words for *world* and multiple meanings for each word. Depending on the word and context in which it appears, they result in at least five different meanings in the

Bible. *World* is used to describe (1) the universe and created order, (2) the scene of human activity, (3) the place or people God desires to save, (4) the fallen race and systems at enmity with God, and (5) a transitory age which will pass away. Knowing which is used in which context is essential to properly applying the meaning of a given text to our life.

Second, God is not only our Savior, but our Creator. It is impossible to overstate the practical importance of recognizing this fact. Because God created humans, we possess an inherent value to God just as our children do for us. This value extends to all humans regardless of their religious beliefs or behavior. Furthermore, because we are created in God's image, all humans, however tainted by sin, reflect traces of a God-given capacity for understanding right and wrong, for relationships, and for creativity in their work. So too, all human cultures reflect the presence of God's image in some way and measure. The planet itself has inherent value as the place God created for human habitation.

Pete's view reduces all uses of the word *world* to one, a people and place at enmity with God, and then ignores God as Creator, focusing only on God as Savior. As a result, human life consists only of "getting saved," "separating yourself from pagans," then hanging on until Jesus returns and God destroys this wretched place.

Pete overlooks what the Reformers referred to as *common grace*, that residual trace of God in all humans endowing them with a sense of right, beauty, and truth. Common grace—this awareness of the shadow of God's image imprinted on all people—enables us to enjoy the good aspects of planet earth, its inhabitants, and its cultures. By ignoring the range of ways the word *world* is used in Scripture and by forgetting the powerful implications of God as the Creator of all humans, Pete and others with his point of view often possess distorted ideas of what God expects of them in the world. This can result in hurtful relationships with and attitudes toward people who don't share their particular perspective, and prohibits them from enjoying the abundant life promised by Jesus.

Given a broader perspective on who God is and what the Bible means by "the world," let me describe three ways God loves the world.

GOD LOVES THE PLANET EARTH

Following each of his creative acts, God said, "It is good." And though tainted by sin, the universe still proclaims the glory and goodness of God.

There was a shepherd, David, a man after God's own heart, who wrote of his experiences in the fields. He likened his thirst for God to the deer he had observed longing for flowing streams. He wrote that "the heavens are telling the glory of God" (Psalm 19:1). Isaiah, another nature lover, wrote about mountains bursting into song and trees clapping their hands (Isaiah 55:12). A contemporary lyricist wrote "This is My Father's World," a song celebrating the Creator's touch on all of nature.

Of all people on earth, we who love God should delight ourselves in the breathtaking beauty and complexity of the universe and the wonder of our own environment on planet earth. Furthermore, God commands us to subdue and manage this planet like a good gardener tends a garden. Why? Because God loves this world—and so should I!

GOD LOVES HUMAN CRAFTMANSHIP AND CREATIVITY

Just as God delighted in his own work saying, "It is good," God also enjoys the expression of human giftedness and craftsmanship. "Do you see those who are skillful in their work? They will serve kings; they will not serve common people" (Proverbs 22:29). Our unique abilities are given by the God who instructed Moses to send for the most talented craftsmen available when building the tabernacle. He said of Bezalel, "I have filled him with divine spirit, with ability, intelligence, and knowledge in every kind of craft" (Exodus 31:3).

Every human possesses a capacity for blessing the rest of us through their devotion to developing the unique genius God has crafted in them. How can we not enjoy the wonder of human creativity when we know it is a gift from God? As Mother Theresa saw Jesus in the poor, so we can see God's image and infinite creativity in the craftsmanlike work of humans whose unique giftedness is from the hand of God himself.

God loves our work because God loves his creative image reflected in us. God loves art and artists, music and musicians, computer programs and programmers, and film and filmmakers. He loves the cooking channel because he loves the chefs (plus he made all the ingredients they use in cooking), he loves the travel channel because he loves explorers (and he created the exotic places they explore). Each type of work is a reflection of a tiny slice of God's infinite capacity for creativity. Like a parent who gushes over the handiwork of a child, posting it on the refrigerator, God is in the business of enjoying the stuff we bring home at day's end. We glorify him with our output. Of all people on earth, we who love God should delight ourselves in the products of human minds, hearts, and hands. Why? Because God loves this world—and so should I!

GOD LOVES THE WORLD OF RELATIONSHIPS

God is exhilarated by human relationships. He loves the loves we manifest: brotherly love, sacrificial love, and erotic love. He loves the laughter and tears of friends. He loves couples united in marriage, pledging a lifetime of devotion to each other. He loves parents protecting their kids and preparing them for their own life adventure. He loves the way we weep at the loss of a departed loved one. All these human experiences spring from

God, who says it is not good that we should be alone, from God who said, let *us* make humankind in our own image. All humans share the inborn need for other humans because God made us that way. Of all people on earth, we who love God should enthusiastically engage in loving, caring relationships. Why? Because God loves this world—and so should I!

GOD LOVES THE WORLD THAT HE CAME TO SAVE

God's love for the planet and our craftsmanship originate in his role as Creator. But God also loves the world as Savior. After Creation came the Fall and the emergence of what God doesn't love in the world: human rebellion. But even our rebellion could not destroy God's love for us. Jesus describes God as a shepherd seeking his lost sheep or a Father yearning for a runaway son. Jesus himself, looking at the crowds, was moved with compassion, for they were like sheep without a shepherd. These images convey love, forgiveness, and acceptance and are quite explicitly not condemning. This is the manner of love God has for "the world."

Anyone following the contemporary human journey should share this same compassion for confused and lost people. Allow me to illustrate with three stories.

Marlo Morgan is a Midwesterner in her fifties whose life was lacking in excitement until she made a trip to Australia, where she alleges she was kidnapped by aborigines who stripped her down and issued her a loin cloth. She claims to have wandered the desert learning from them thirty thousand years of ancient wisdom. She returned and told her story in *Mutant Message Down Under*, and sold it to a publisher as nonfiction.

When the publisher couldn't verify any part of her story as true, they required her to publish it as fiction. I asked her about this and she told me she didn't care because "what is true for me is true for me, and what is true for you is true for you!" It reminds me of the cartoon where Ziggy stands in a bookstore in front of three bookshelves. One says "Fiction," the second says "Nonfiction," and the third says "Not sure!" Don't you feel compassion for Marlo Morgan and the hundreds of thousands of people who bought her book hoping it would fill their spiritual void?

Eddie Stierle joined the Joffrey Ballet in 1986. At eighteen he was the company's youngest member. A reviewer of his biography reports sadly, "Born into a working-class Catholic family, Stierle found it impossible to reconcile his religion with his homosexuality. Unwilling to abandon his faith in a higher authority, he replaced his Catholic God with a nonjudgmental God. Eventually Stierle became a follower of Marianne Williamson, author of the best-selling *A Course in Miracles*, and some of the saddest pages in *A Dance Against Time* describe his pitiful floundering in the ankle-deep spiritual waters of the New Age movement. Williamson ... advised him to envision the AIDS virus as a gentle, loving being dressed in fearsome armor ... Williamson preferred her own version of the AIDS acronym, 'Angels in Darth Vader suits.'"

Stierle died not long thereafter. Doesn't his sad story move you to compassion?

Among the recent examples of spiritual confusion is the late Princess Di, revered by so many, yet so lonely and openly seeking. Weeks before her death she took Dodi to meet her psychic. *Time* reported that the psychic had once tried to put Diana in touch with her dead father. The psychic was only one of many of Princess Di's attempts to find personal peace. Diana, suffering from a series of emotional disorders (bulimia, self-mutilation), had consulted astrologers and various psychotherapists over the years. At one time or another, she had also tried aromatherapy, acupuncture, colonic irrigation, holistic massage, mud therapy, reflexology, and energy healing.

This beautiful woman, memorialized as a candle in the wind, was spiritually adrift. She is not untypical of so many people today, searching but never finding, on a spiritual journey without a clear destination.

Can you listen to these stories and not be moved with compassion for lost, deceived, and fallen people? Do you weep for them like Jesus wept for the harassed people of his day? Do we dare stand in judgment of them as if we should benefit from the wideness of God's mercy and they should not?

Instead of love and compassion, today's seeker often sees in Christians only a self-righteous judgmentalism of the type displayed by Pete when he called my show. Dean Merrill captured the nature of the problem brilliantly in the title of his recent book, *Sinners in the Hands of an Angry Church*. John Ortberg says, "The first casualty of the culture war isn't truth. It is love." People like Pete actually justify not loving people. They argue that their commitment to holiness means they can't associate with people like Eddie Stierle, or that associating with gays is tantamount to consorting with the enemy. Instead of loving a woman who is deceived by a "mutant message from down under," they might attack her or mock her because of the weirdness of her beliefs.

When we lose our first love and forget our true marching orders, we begin to take comfort in our holy pieties. We rise to do battle with people for whom Jesus died. We attack the theologically deceived instead of lovingly correcting them. We circle our wagons to protect ourselves, keeping seekers out instead of breaking camp and living among them.

Jesus summarized our calling to love the world this way. "'Love the Lord your God with all your heart, and with all your soul, and with all your strength, and with all your mind; and your neighbor as yourself'" (Luke 10:27).

And so our love and devotion to God fully engages us in a love for the world. We love the world as a miraculous place God created, as a display case of human work and creativity, and as the scene of God's love story toward rebellious humans.

Live life fully! Love the world!

CHAPTER 5

BE A TRUE FRIEND

A RECENT CARTOON SHOWS A NURSE wheeling a patient out of his room. "Relax, Mr. Harbst," she says, "we're moving you from intensive care to indifferent care." Years ago sociologist David Reisman described Americans as the "lonely crowd." In his book, *Connect*, Harvard Medical School's Dr. Edward Hallowell says loneliness is epidemic today and is the by-product of a society in which most people lack any substantial connection with someone who cares and listens attentively. Many people are lonely, and the result is a crying need for friends who will slow down, listen, and care.

This epidemic of loneliness offers a great opportunity to serve people, because one of the most effective ways to take Jesus into your world is to simply be a friend to a person who needs one. But our too-pagan, too-Christian paradox presents some interesting problems when applied to our friendships.

PROBLEM #1: MANY CHRISTIANS HAVE NO PAGAN FRIENDS

Many who are "too Christian" have never taken the time to nurture friendships with "pagans" because they have spent so much of their time hanging out with other Christians. My friend Alex the anthropologist is an example.

Alex fancies himself a skeptic, introvert, and benign curmudgeon. Raised in a nominally Christian home, his conversion came in high school by way of a fundamentalism that taught him to see everybody in the world in two distinct groups—*us* (born-again Christians), and *them* (pagans needing to be converted). This "us versus them" view of the world leads to a multitude of distortions in life, not the least of which is our friendships, and in college Alex found himself frustrated with his Christian roommate's choice of friends.

As leader of a campus Bible study, Alex was responsible for recruiting other leaders. Alex's new roommate, Mark, was the ideal candidate. To an introvert like Alex, having the ideal recruit assigned to share a dorm room with a reticent recruiter seemed to be divinely inspired. Alas, Mark did not see it this way, because he had already allocated his spare time to working at the college radio station.

Let me assure you, Bible study is the last thing you'll find at the typical college radio station. College radio stations are commonly staffed by the grandest assortment of oddballs and ne'er-do-wells known unto man. They are often dreamers, whackos, and quirky Neanderthals, young Howard Sterns waiting to be discovered. To Alex, these people seemed unworthy of Mark's attention, especially when compared to the opportunity of joining him and his stellar compatriots in studying the blessed and holy Word of God. Nevertheless, Mark would not be dissuaded from his broadcasting pursuits, a decision which left Alex sorely vexed in spirit.

Poor Alex had no idea his negative view about friendships with pagans was about to be shaken up. It happened one quiet evening when Mark and Alex were studying. At about 10 P.M., who should appear at their door but the radio raga-muffins from the station. "We're here to kidnap you," they shouted to Mark. And with hoots and hollers and various other auditory disturbances to the placid stillness of the night, they did just that. Alex wondered what this was all about. "Up to no good they are," thought Alex, returning to his lofty academic pursuits.

The next morning Alex asked, "So what was that all about last night?"

Mark replied, "Oh, they wanted to surprise me for my birthday."

Confirmed in his suspicions that these radio guys were truly and completely clueless, Alex responded smugly, "But your birthday isn't for three months."

"Oh, not *that* birthday," said Mark without guile. "They were celebrating my *spiritual* birthday!"

Alex recalled that when the guys from the station arrived they were hiding what looked like a cake complete with four lit candles. And he remembered that just four years earlier Mark had made his decision to follow Jesus. Immediately Alex realized that while he was off *studying* the truth needed by "heathens," his friend Mark was actually *living this truth* among them in compelling ways. Instantly Alex knew that any heathen could not be all bad who would celebrate a friend's "born-again" birthday though claiming no spiritual life or interest in one himself. Alex began his slow sojourn out of an "us-versus-them" fundamentalism into genuine friendships with pagans.

PROBLEM #2: MANY CHRISTIANS BEFRIEND PAGANS ONLY TO TRY TO CONVERT THEM

Some people who are too Christian befriend pagans only because they intend to convert them. This brings us to Alex's second story. Having himself evolved from a mindset in which sinners were not friends, but rather targets for evangelism, Alex found himself engaged in conversation with a certain evangelistically motivated fellow named Rick, regarding his practice of playing racquetball with pagans. No longer believing friendships with pagans to be inadvisable, Alex simply wanted to commend his friend for this activity.

Rick was straightforward regarding his motivation. He wanted to "win these guys for Christ." This is certainly a worthy desire. But what, wondered Alex, is the true nature of the relationship in such a situation? And so Alex, keen of mind and full of curiosity, asked a profound question. "Rick, if you knew beyond a shadow of a doubt that not one of these guys would ever become a Christian, would you continue playing racquetball with them?" Given the seriousness of the question, Alex was surprised at the rapidity and intensity of the reply. "Absolutely not," Rick said. Further discussion revealed Rick's belief that his sole purpose on earth was to fulfill the Great Commission, and any investment of time that could not contribute to this purpose was vain and frivolous.

Before criticizing Rick, I want you to stop for a moment and ask yourself if you share Rick's passion for the lost. It is commendable and all too rare among today's disciples.

But I also want to acknowledge the trap laid for those of us who are type-A, goal-oriented, management-by-objective achievers. Given our evangelistic zeal, we can view people as targets for our efforts instead of relating to them as fellow humans created in God's image. We are embarrassingly capable of becoming ministry machines, clustering people into categories and then intentionally organizing our time with them to accomplish our purposes.

This happened to me early in my life with Jesus. After starting as a "don't ask, don't tell" Christian, I swung to the other extreme and became totally calculating and strategic in my passion to share Jesus with my friends. As presumptuous as it sounds, I would invite people for dinner and then prior to their arrival would think through where they were in their walk and where they should be. I would then develop communication goals for the evening. The joy of relationships became dulled by the obsessive-compulsiveness of a well-intentioned but misdirected Christian. Eventually I realized that relationships are spontaneous and grow out of the serendipity of long, aimless stretches of time with another human. I then understood that a calculating and mission-driven Christian often is not a very good friend at all.

PROBLEM #3: MANY CHRISTIANS DO NOT INFLUENCE THEIR PAGAN FRIENDS

While being too intentional is probably worse than having no pagan friends, an even worse situation is presented by the Christians with numerous pagan friends whom they don't influence spiritually at all. Rick was too obsessive and intentional with his racquetball partners, but at least they knew he was concerned about their spiritual well-being. Many of us have friendships with pagan friends who know nothing of our spiritual convictions because we've retreated into a "don't ask, don't tell" policy about our faith. Someday we will give an accounting for our silence with our friends.

This year I received an e-mail that makes the point well. It was from an acquaintance I knew in high school in the sixties. Eric was listening to my talk show and heard me mention graduating from Fullerton High School. He wondered if I might be the same humorous, fun-loving Dick Staub he remembered from the good old days in Southern California. We began an e-mail reunion in which I learned that after wasting his life in riotous living in the sixties, he became a Christian in the seventies. Most sobering to me was the fact that after he became a believer, he *suspected* I was a Christian back in those days, *but did not know for sure*. Here is his e-mail.

Just thinking about you today. Got caught in a nostalgic flow of our youth. I know you are busy, but if you get some time, I have a few questions. You got saved while we were still in high school, right? What were the wild "turn on, tune in, and drop out" days like as a Christian? Seeing from the spiritual side of things it must have blown your mind to see the major deception that was going on. I unfortunately was still very lost, therefore consumed in the humanistic thinking of the day (surf, sun, sex, drugs, and rock 'n' roll). Did it seem like Sodom and Gomorrah? What was going on in the church? Was the Word being preached, or was it just formalized Christianity? Did you pray for us in those days? Did you expect God to really answer? Did He give you hope for your generation? Signs and wonders?

Did you find a great deal of discouragement? I didn't even hear about Jesus until around '71, and I was so consumed with self, I rejected Him. I know now there were prayers being made for us raunchy characters. I don't really remember you saying anything to me in the sixties, but I do remember you being a clean-cut kid, one with a noncursing mouth. You may have tried to witness to me, but I was dead and didn't hear you.

These may be some hard questions to answer, because so much time has passed. I am ashamed of my wasted youth, but am now greatly and gloriously filled with joy because Jesus is my Lord.

If you have opportunity, please answer these questions. I would like to know what I missed out on.

I committed my life to Jesus between my junior and senior year of high school, so in one of our four years together I undoubtedly had opportunities to share Jesus with Eric, but I'm ashamed to say, I doubt that I did. I was one of those don't ask, don't tell Christians who was fortunate enough that Eric discovered Jesus despite me!

BEING A TRUE FRIEND

So we've observed three bad models: (1) the Christian with no pagan friends, (2) the Christian who has pagan friends only because he hopes to convert them, and (3) the Christian with pagan friends who has no spiritual influence on their life. There must be a better way. There is. Let's call it being a true friend.

A true friend allows a relationship to grow naturally out of daily activities and interests. God will direct you toward new friends, and you don't need to strategize or force it. Sooner or later you'll find a friendship developing. How will you recognize it? The dictionary says a friend is "a person you know, like, and trust." A true friend can be counted on. Carole King's Grammy award-winning song says:

> When you're down, in trouble,
> And you need some loving care,
> And nothing, nothing is going right . . .
> Winter, spring, summer, or fall,
> All you've got to do is call—
> I'll be there . . .
> You've got a friend.

They're there when you're down or in trouble, or when you just need a kind word. A true friend is there in the good times and the bad. A true friend is accepting even when disapproving of a friend's bad decisions or behavior. Sticking with someone even when you think he is headed down an idiotic path is an important mark of friendship. Friendships conditioned on approval are less durable than friendships "for better or for worse." This is difficult when your friend is violating spiritual laws that you know will only reap unhappiness, but just as you cannot force someone to take care of his physical body, you cannot force him to take care of his soul.

But a true friendship is also based on honesty, disagreements, and tough discussions. A friend is someone who has earned the right to be heard. There will come times in your friendship when you will be given an opportunity to share your faith.

The apostle Peter describes the progression this way. First, you conduct yourself in an exemplary manner (1 Peter 2:12). Peter says some people will be won over without a word, simply by watching your behavior (1 Peter 3:1). Second, always be ready to make your defense to anyone who demands from you an accounting for the hope that is within you (1 Peter 3:15), yet do it with gentleness and reverence. With one of my friends, the breakthrough came when he realized he wanted somebody to pray for a situation he was facing and I was the only person he knew who could pray with him. Another friend of ours was grieving the death of her mother and wanted to know what happens to people after they die. Another friend decided he wanted to start talking about spiritual stuff while packed into a bus on the way to a college football game.

How do you get ready for these moments? Pray for your friend. Listen so you know in advance the kinds of issues your friend may want to discuss. In the very moment your friend opens the door for discussion, pray and ask God to guide you toward saying just the right things. Jesus promised we would get this kind of help. "Do not worry about how you are to speak or what you are to say; for what you are to say will be given to you at that time; for it is not you who speak, but the Spirit of your Father speaking through you" (Matthew 10:19–20).

Many people can be a friend, but the truest of friends is a lover of a friend's soul. That is how Jesus is described in one of my favorite old hymns.

> Jesus what a friend for sinners,
>   Jesus lover of my soul;
> Friends may fail me, foes assail me,
>   he my Savior makes me whole.
> Jesus what a strength in weakness
>   let me hide myself in him;
> Tempted, tried, and sometimes failing,
>   he my strength my victory wins.
> Jesus what a help in sorrow,
>   while the billows o'er me roll;
> Even when my heart is breaking,
>   he my comfort helps my soul.
> Jesus what a guide and keeper,
>   while the tempest still is high;
> Storms about me, night o'er takes me,
>   he my pilot hears my cry.

If you truly desire to be more effective taking Jesus into your world, one of the best places to start is to simply be the kind of friend Jesus is. And Jesus is a friend for sinners. The hymn says he is a friend because he is a "lover of my soul." There is a difference between someone who wants only to win your soul, and someone who loves your soul. One will play racquetball with you no matter what; the other won't. The hymn says Jesus is a friend because he "makes me whole." Since creation we have known deep down in our primordial beings that when alone we are incomplete. Made for relationship with God and others, our souls are restless until they find their rest in relationship with God and others. A friend loves your soul.

Friends often like to introduce old friends to their new ones. So there is nothing inconsistent with you hoping to introduce your friends to your truest friend, Jesus. When that happens you are providing your friend with a great opportunity to become friends with the God of the universe. Then, along with you, your friend can sing:

> Jesus, I do now receive him,
>   more than all in him I find;
> He hath granted me forgiveness,
>   I am his and he is mine.
> Hallelujah! What a Savior! Hallelujah!
>   What a friend!
> Saving, helping, keeping, loving,
>   he is with me to the end.

Be a friend. Be there as a friend. Pray. Live an honorable life. Be patient.

God will bless it.

CHAPTER 6

CROSS CULTURES

HAVING ESTABLISHED THE IMPORtance of friendship, I must remind you that though your primary circle of influence is with your friends, your influence should not be limited to them. If you follow Jesus' example, you will expand your circle of influence into relationships with people outside your familiar group and very different from you. This stretching across cultural boundaries requires a level of commitment, adaptation, and elasticity clearly modeled by Jesus and needed badly by today's disciples.

It is often observed that Jesus engaged the truly marginalized or disenfranchised in his culture. The poor, lepers, tax collectors, drunkards, women—all found themselves drawn into the inner circle of Jesus' love, attention, and affection. In a society characterized by distinctions of race and class, this required crossing cultural barriers and breaking the taboos of the day's religious subculture. For instance, in the first century many devout people believed they could not be holy if they touched an unclean person like a leper. So when Jesus reached out to touch a leper, he surprised the leper and offended the devout. Jesus spent so much of his time crossing these kinds of barriers that on one occasion the Pharisees asked Jesus' disciples, "Why does your teacher eat with tax collectors and sinners?" (Matthew 9:11).

Jesus, overhearing the question, said, "Those who are well have no need of a physician, but those who are sick. Go and learn what this means: 'I desire mercy, not sacrifice.' For I have come to call not the righteous but sinners" (Matthew 9:12–13). This teaching and example was one of the hardest for the Pharisees to grasp, and is difficult for many Christians to grasp today as well. It is much easier to stay within our cultural comfort zones than to venture into groups of people whose behavior violates traditional religious norms. When respectable religious folks criticize our venturing forth, it is even more difficult. However, it seems clear that to follow Jesus' example means you will cross cultural barriers to demonstrate love to the disenfranchised and marginalized. This is easy to say and very difficult to do.

Dwight Ozard puts it bluntly:

The greatest mission field we face is not in some faraway land. The strange and foreign culture most Americans fear is not across the ocean. It's barely across the street. The culture most lost to the gospel is our own—our children and neighbors. It's a culture that can't say two sentences without referencing a TV show or a pop song. . . . It's a culture more likely to have a body part pierced than to know why Sarah laughed. It's a culture that we stopped loving and declared a culture war upon.

Thinking about Jesus' ministry to the marginalized and Dwight's words about pierced body parts reminded me of a conversation with a very dear and close friend. My wife and I were at Joanne's home for a barbecue. She was telling us about their family outing to Great America amusement park, complaining about the raunchiness of the crowds with their skimpy tank tops, "F" word every-other-word language, nose rings, and purple hair. They were loud, pushy, and obnoxious. "We just wanted to have fun with our kids, and we have to put up with this! It's ridiculous!" she complained.

Just a few years earlier Joanne and her husband had spent a few years voluntarily living and working among a primitive tribal group, so her derisive attitude toward the "unreached people" she encountered at Great America seemed inconsistent to me. With her husband egging me on, I good-naturedly and vigorously exposed the manifest dissonance of Joanne's nasty remarks about the local "heathen." As family members gathered, apparently tired of badminton and eager to see what controversy the aging talk show host might spark, I explored with our hostess the reasons for her impatience with our local heathen given her track record of service to the "heathen" abroad.

THE "I'M GETTING TOO OLD FOR THIS" ARGUMENT

This one was actually advanced by me as a preemptive strike, lest my own inconsistencies be revealed as a deflection from her behavior. I pointed out that on my first trip abroad I was nineteen and more than eager to see and experience all the world had to offer. Indonesia, site of my first international adventure, offered a veritable feast of exotic opportunities. I wore a sarong, the skirt-like garment favored by traditional

Javanese. In place of toilet paper, I employed the local Balinese substitute, a corncob in the field. I ate bugs, snakes, and ox tail. In Kalimantan I drank a local soft drink bottled with a ceremonial worm to be slurped down when reaching the bottom of the jug. I listened attentively as the Balinese performed their *ketjak*, or "monkey dance." It involves over seventy men sitting in concentric circles calling out a cacophonous, staccato chant and then suddenly morphing into a subdued trance while masked actors enter the circle to play out their drama. The actors deliver their lines, not with words, but with other-than-human squeaks and squawks until the chanting begins again and they exit the stage. I screamed maniacally with the crowd of short, sweaty men packed into a bamboo-walled arena to watch a cruel, bloody cockfight. In Bali I followed a Hindu funeral procession complete with a pyre looking strangely like a Rose Parade float, with its decorative, life-sized papier-mâché bull. I was a vagabond in search of authentic ethnic otherness, and I found all that and more.

By nature and from youth, I've possessed a natural curiosity and fondness for diversity even here in the United States. However (and what I'm about to tell you pains me), as an older man, I find myself occasionally irritated with differences, yearning for predictability, weary of being entertained by deviations from the norm. Sometimes I feel that I've seen "the world," and now I want to just enjoy "my world," thank you very much!

The hostess did not buy this argument, I think on two counts. First, she was unwilling to grant, and what woman would, that her age was either advancing or affecting her in any observable way. And she especially did not want to grant this in the presence of her children, ever vigilant in their quest to demonstrate another teenage absolute: parental obtuseness and "motherly-out-of-touchness."

Second, and this is more nuanced, most of us imagine that with time and life experience, we will become more mature, not less. And certainly, irritability toward blue hair and nose rings does not seem the height of maturity, but instead, seems rather petty. And so, we left the age issue and moved on to another possible explanation for missionarian crabbiness.

THE INTENTIONALITY "I'M HERE TO MINISTER" ISSUE

Joanne gamely advanced the argument that, because she sallied forth to Great America in search of fun, while she'd been in "primitive country xyz" to minister, she couldn't be expected to display the same patience with tribe A as she had with tribe B.

In short, she contended that in one setting she was working and in the other she was on vacation. This, of course, drew my thoughts to our model of effective ministry, Jesus. Did Jesus ever take time off to just have fun? Granted, we offer only conjecture on Jesus' recreational life, because the biblical record is relatively silent on the matter. We know he believed in a day of rest. We also know that his culture derived its greatest recreational pleasure from small social gatherings, eating meals, and conversing with a circle of family and close friends.

Studying Jesus' life, we see that he did, at times, get away from it all. Unfortunately, for Joanne's argument, there are no recorded instances of Jesus taking "time off" while in a crowd. One doubts such a notion would have occurred to him. Jesus' time off seems to have been taken alone. He would arise a great while before the day, or at day's end might enjoy a balmy boat ride on the Sea of Galilee with a few close friends. It is hard to imagine Jesus gathering a few of his disciples, paying the price of admission at Great America, and upon encountering the cross-cultural masses saying to them, "Yo, get outta here, we earth boys just wanna have fun." We would conclude that Jesus understood rest is essential, practiced by God at creation and commanded by God in the Ten

Commandments. However, it seems Jesus felt he had a responsibility when he was with others to be available to engage them for God's glory.

I DIDN'T THINK OF IT AS A CROSS-CULTURAL SITUATION

Our hostess, despite her clearly superior understanding of cross-cultural dynamics, confessed that she really hadn't thought of her aggravations as rooted in cultural differences. From time to time each of us fall into the subtle trap of thinking cross-cultural encounters take place only in foreign countries or when crossing ethnic lines. The truth is, America's melting pot no longer (if it ever did) produces a uniform stew. Nose rings, language, dress, musical taste, even volume can be reflections of cultural differences found coexisting in most American cities. On our Naperville street you'd find recent immigrants from China, India, and Pakistan. You'd find first-generation Irish and Italian. There were those raised in urban Chicago living next to those raised on rural Illinois farms living adjacent to those whose only experience is upscale suburban living. In America our everyday encounters are increasingly cross-cultural.

Here again Jesus' life is informative. At one level, all of Jesus' ministry was cross-cultural because he was fully God and fully man surrounded by mere mortals. We know enough about Jesus' own cultural milieu to agree on certain basics. Jesus was a Jewish man, born in Bethlehem, raised in Nazareth in a God-fearing, carpenter's home. He was not a Pharisee, Sadducee, or Herodian. He was not a woman. He was not a Roman, Greek, or Samaritan. He was not a tax collector, lawyer, or fisherman. Every day he awakened to a world of cultural diversity and headed out to remind people of their common roots in God his Father. He expects no less of us.

By now the conversation, though friendly and light-hearted, was turning serious, and badminton was again looking scintillating for the kids. But there was one more point to be explored. When the veneer of our universal cross-cultural incompetence is peeled away, it can be exposed as our core problem.

CROSS-CULTURAL MINISTRY IS HARD WORK

Crossing cultural barriers requires listening, observing, learning a different language, and understanding different customs and traditions. It can mean eating different foods. It is hard work. Whether because we're old or lazy, we'd often rather not exert the effort to coexist, let alone truly relish daily life with people unlike us.

And here we face some basic truths. All people are created in the image of God, and most cultural diversities represent preferences, not irreconcilable differences. Seen in this way, our cultural diversities reflect the infinite creativity and rich variety God evidently finds enjoyable and full of potential for glorifying Him. All cultures are not equally glorifying to God, because every culture, including our own, is tainted in varying degrees with the pollutants of sin. But there is to be found, even in the most off-putting cultural expressions, a kernel of God's image trying to shine through, no matter how bent and distorted its presentation. I believe this is why Jesus was able to get past the demoniac's repulsiveness and restore him to his right mind. It is why Jesus saw a person in the woman at the well, or the woman caught in adultery. It is why he touched the leper. It is why he was so effective with diverse people from a whole range of cultures. It is why he is able to love you and me.

"Image of God in them" is one piece of the cross-cultural effectiveness puzzle. And, not to be trite, for us, the "cross" is the other piece of the puzzle. A daily willingness to do the work of crossing cultures requires dying to self and to familiar cultural preferences. Looking for God's image in other people may fuel our curiosity and intrigue us, but only the cross will sustain the process of crossing cultural barriers. The moral of the story is an important one for those of us who want to follow Jesus and to take him into our world—the follower of Jesus can get cross at cultural differences, or we can cross them.

CHAPTER 7

■ GO TO THE PARTY

I RECENTLY ATTENDED A WEDDING OF a young couple who invited their evangelical pastor to perform the wedding ceremony alongside their mainline denominational pastor. It seemed clear that the evangelical felt duty bound to improve the spiritual development of the couple, families, and guests in attendance. His remarks were carefully chosen, appropriate, and delivered well, but his impact that evening was diminished by one seemingly insignificant decision.

He apparently decided his work was complete when the ceremony was finished and was therefore notably absent at the reception, an elegant and extravagant celebration set exquisitely at a local country club. In my view he made the classic error of thinking ministry happens at church but not at the party. How many movies have you seen featuring what happened at the reception after the wedding? People solemnly watch the ceremony, but the party after the wedding is festive and relational. Jesus understood this and seemed to spend considerable time at meals and parties hosted by pagans.

Let me ask a question. Do you like to go to pagan parties?

You might say no because you are quite uncomfortable at pagan parties. You know bad things can happen there. When alcohol flows freely or drugs are involved, things can spin quickly out of control. The jokes, the language, the sexual innuendo—it all adds up to an uncomfortable experience for somebody trying to live a transformed life. And the raunch is starting young. In Colorado a thirty-five-year-old father was arrested for hiring a stripper for his twelve-year-old's birthday party. When questioned by police, he said, "I just wanted to be a cool dad."

I was raised in a very conservative family, so going to wild parties was not part of my upbringing. The world with all its charms was considered evil, and holiness meant remaining separate from the world. While not literally separate like the Amish, our tradition tried to identify activities considered worldly and behaviorally off limits. The length of these informal lists would differ—the filthy five, the sinful seven, the nasty nine, or the dirty dozen. On the list were things like drinking, swearing, smoking, and gambling. They might include what many people considered harmless activities like dancing, playing cards, or attending the movies. If you were raised in that kind of background, when attending parties you may be haunted by voices from your past admonishing you to "abstain from every form of evil" (1 Thessalonians 5:22) or warning you that "friendship with the world is enmity with God" (James 4:4).

Fear of the party is not all bad. If you were raised in a "let the good times roll" kind of background, your memory may be filled with recollections of wild, downward-spiraling situations you want to avoid repeating. As a transformed person your appetites have changed, and you want to stay away from the party scene.

Other professing Christians love to party and seem to have no problem fitting into even the most extreme and unruly settings. They say, "Of coarse I like pagan parties, especially compared to the dull, pent-up people I meet at church parties."

How would *I* answer the question "Do you like to go to pagan parties?" My answer would be "It depends."

I know bad things can happen at parties, but because I want God to govern my life, I am determined to follow Jesus even outside my comfort zones. My decision about a pagan party depends on whether Jesus wants me there or not, and that depends on whether I can be an effective presence for Jesus there. In short, I like to be at the party if Jesus wants me there.

There is no question that at times Jesus partied with pagans. Early in his ministry Jesus sat down at dinner with many tax collectors and sinners (Matthew 9:10). The edginess of these parties is hinted at by the criticisms Jesus received for being there: "The Son of Man came eating and drinking, and they say, 'Look, a glutton and a drunkard, a friend of tax collectors and sinners'" (Matthew 11:19).

The question is not *did* Jesus party with pagans, but *why*.

Jesus answered that question when the Pharisees criticized him for attending these parties. Jesus said, "Those who are well have no need of a physician, but those who are sick" (Matthew 9:12). Jesus was at the party because that is where the sick people are!

Jesus understood that eating meals together can foster a camaraderie and intimacy conducive to people opening up and talking freely with each other.

Jesus spent a lot of time at parties, because he loved people and knew God could do good things in these settings. His first public miracle occurred at a wedding reception where he turned water into wine. Another miracle occurred when Jesus visited the house of Zacchaeus, a diminutive and despised tax collector. Zacchaeus was so moved by Jesus' love and acceptance, he gave half his possessions to the poor!

If we are truly following Jesus, I think we will go to some of the parties. It is part of our obedience to Jesus.

What about the warnings I heard in my youth? What about the verses implying that we should not associate with the world? Each of these should be understood in their context.

The warning about not fellowshiping with darkness (2 Corinthians 6:14) is part of Paul's admonition to Corinthian Christians who in word and deed were failing to acknowledge their distinctiveness from the pagan culture around them and were allowing the world to pollute the church. By trying to harmonize cultural immorality with Christian living, the Corinthians were forging a cooperative partnership and fellowship of the two. Paul is telling them this is impossible. Paul has already specifically told these Christians he does not want them out of the world (1 Corinthians 5:9–10); now in 2 Corinthians 6, he is admonishing them to keep worldly behavior out of their personal and church life because the two are incompatible. (I'll expand on this in Chapter 8, "Avoid the Corinthian Syndrome.")

Sometimes people say that to avoid the very "appearance of evil" (1 Thessalonians 5:22 KJV) means we should avoid even physical proximity to evil. Scholars now tell us this was a King James Version mistranslation, corrected in the New International Version to read "avoid every kind of evil," thus referring to *committing any kind of evil act.*

The phrase "friendship with the world is enmity with God" (James 4:4) clearly refers to a giving in to our evil cravings and appetites and is not commanding us to avoid friendships with people in the world.

These texts cannot accurately be interpreted to define holiness as abandonment or separation or withdrawal from the world, nor can they be used to define proximity to the profane as inevitably polluting to us. They are, however, useful warnings about the importance of exercising discernment.

Here are some suggested guidelines as you wrestle through the very practical dilemmas posed by parties.

GO WITH A PURPOSE OR DON'T GO AT ALL

Before every party, I try to remember I am going for some purpose which God will reveal in due time. In some particularly dicey situations I've asked friends to pray with me before and during the party.

USE DISCERNMENT

Use discernment in deciding whether or not to attend a party and when to leave.

One company I worked for in San Francisco was renowned for hard partying and pushing the envelope. Prior to an after-hours, by-invitation birthday party I learned that one of the guys had hired two lesbians to come and "perform" on our conference room table. I sent a birthday gift but declined the invitation.

The same company reserved a private waterfront room at a posh Sausalito restaurant for a company-wide event complete with open bar, lunch, and an invitation to stay and party into the early evening. By late afternoon the liquor had flowed long and hard and, among other things, an otherwise timid coworker had shed her inhibitions along with some of her clothes. I knew it was time to leave, and I did.

BE A POSITIVE PRESENCE

Be there as a positive presence and, unless specifically directed by God, not as a critic or judge of behavior. When I am at a party I expect pagans to act like pagans, so I understand they may get drunk, their language might offend, their jokes could cross the line. The apostle Paul warned us what to expect when describing the works of the flesh: "fornication, impurity, licentiousness, idolatry, sorcery, enmities, strife, jealousy, anger, quarrels, dissensions, factions, envy, drunkenness, carousing, and things like these" (Galatians 5:19). Seldom do I feel it is my role as a guest at a party to publicly rail against people's behavior, although I have on many occasions taken a personal friend aside to urge him to curb behavior I know he will regret later.

In these situations, I believe I am called to be a loving presence and blessing in whatever way I can. This means being a presence for the fruit of the Holy Spirit: "love, joy, peace, patience, kindness, generosity, faithfulness, gentleness, and self-control" (Galatians 5:22).

At the party I always assume that underneath the frivolity and riotous behavior are human beings carrying the sorrow and pain that accompanies life without God. I wait for God to reveal how I can serve. This usually involves pulling away from the crowd for a quiet, private conversation with an individual who wants to talk more seriously.

For example, once at a Christmas party I was talking with a man and woman who were new to our neighborhood. He was loud and boisterous and she was poised and genteel. He asked what I did for a living. I told him after years of hosting a national talk show, I became convinced people were on a spiritual journey and so I decided to launch a radio show and a Web site to help them. After some interesting conversation he left to refresh their drinks. She said quickly and softly under her breath, "I'm not married to Rick, and I just put my fifteen-year-old on the plane to go see his real daddy." The mere mention of "spirituality" triggered feelings she wanted to talk about.

REMEMBER GOD'S LOVE FOR THE LOST

Be constantly mindful, people need the Lord, and God loves these people.

There are times I would rather stay home than head out to a party knowing the energy it consumes to be vigilant and discerning. I also know that as intentional as I want to be, sometimes I have been more on the "in the world" side of the ledger than on the "not of the world" side. As my editor wrote in the margin of one draft of this chapter, "Going to parties is not for the faint of heart; going into the world does not excuse us from stupidity." And this issue, more than others, will leave you seeming too pagan for your Christian friends and too Christian for your pagan friends.

So why go to parties? Because God loves people, and people need the Lord. You have decided to follow Jesus, no turning back, no turning back. See you at the party.

CHAPTER 8

■ AVOID THE CORINTHIAN SYNDROME

HAVING URGED YOU TO LOVE THE world and go to the party, I now must advise you of the dangers of following that good but dangerous advice. There are inherent risks in going into the world. Earlier we talked about loving the world, but there is a world we are not to love and it reveals itself in two forms: (1) the fallen human race and systems at enmity with God and (2) the illusory transitory age which will pass away. Perhaps the greatest danger the disciple faces in taking Jesus into the world is the powerful gravitational pull toward the dark side itself. Here is a cautionary tale about one of many who not only *seemed* too pagan but *became* too pagan.

THE STORY OF JOE

Many Christians enter the professional world with the intention of being there for Jesus. But too many of us end up succeeding professionally but hitting the reef spiritually. Joe was such a man. The owner of a successful ad agency in Chicago, Joe and I were introduced by a mutual friend who knew Joe wanted and needed help

At our first dinner together, we connected immediately. Joe was an intelligent, quick-witted, widely read, Type-A Renaissance man with a zest for life. He, like me, possessed a passion for good food as evidenced by the ample storehouse snugly cinched by a strained and ever-tightening belt. When the conversation turned to his spiritual journey, his mood changed. He leaned quietly into the table to tell me his story.

Joe became a believer while a university student, and eventually joined the staff of the student ministry instrumental in his own spiritual awakening. Aware of God's call into the world, Joe concluded that earning professional respect was the path to a credible witness and the right to be heard on matters of faith.

He entered the world of advertising where his creativity and talents led to a fast track upward through the ranks of a well established firm, winning awards and earning a reputation for his national campaigns. As the firm grew, its creative edge dulled, and eventually one of his clients convinced Joe to go out on his own. He did, and began surpassing the creative and financial success of his previous venture. He was very hot.

But his success was exacting a price. From the beginning, given his desire to influence coworkers for the kingdom, he felt he needed to identify with them rather than judge them. Unfortunately, more and more he found himself behaving just like them. He frequently entertained out-of-town clients who wanted a good time in the big city. He felt it was his obligation to show them one, so he did.

Their definition of "good time" crossed many lines he had set prior to entering the business. He began drinking heavily, sometimes taking clients to topless bars, justifying his presence there professionally as the "cost of doing business," and spiritually as following Jesus where the sinners are. Eventually he dropped the spiritual rationalization and concentrated on building a successful business, and soon found himself feeling no need to justify what he was doing, because he liked what he was doing and where it was taking him.

Perhaps even more problematic, he found his work and coworkers eminently more exhilarating than the mundane matters awaiting him at home with his wife and three kids. To his long weekday hours, he added weekend "client development" outings that were often really nothing more than a way for him to enjoy weekend excursions on the company account, in the presence of people who understood him and found him exceedingly entertaining. His family, on the other hand, was exceedingly irritated with him. To Joe, of course, this meant they were unappreciative and lacking in imagination. After all, he was providing for their every need and desire. What more did they want?

Having begun this business venture with the advice of a spiritual accountability group, Joe became too busy to meet his buddies for the weekly breakfast. Always discontent with the church because it lacked a concern for reaching the world, Joe had developed sophisticated arguments for why the visible church wasn't the real church anyway. He argued that the real church was a remnant of rebels who understood the gospel as a party for outsiders instead of a pristine club for suburban, upwardly mobile types. Wanting no part of the upscale, pious, suburban sham that called itself his local church, Joe withdrew and at one point even started his own gathering for unchurched types. It quickly deteriorated from a "party with a purpose" to just a party.

Rich, our mutual friend, stuck with Joe through it all. He figured, "If God doesn't give up on people, neither will I." Plus, he enjoyed Joe and loved him. I could see why. Joe is the kind of guy you want to be around, because wherever Joe is things happen. Joe knew a lot of funny stories and told them well. He was the rare drinker who grew more cheerful and exuberant as the evening wore on. The people who worked with Joe felt like they were getting paid for having fun! Between his extraordinary talent and high-spirited personality, it was clear to me why his business was a success.

But Rich knew Joe was at a dangerous crossroads. Underneath the festive facade, Joe was being eaten up by his conscience and the awareness that his professional gains were resulting in spiritual ruin for him and his family. His high school daughter, apple of his eye, had just told him she was pregnant. She'd been at an all-night after-prom party, got drunk, and ended up sleeping with a football player. Joe faced the very real possibility of losing his marriage. His wife had pretty well had it with his cavalier, "I love you guys but gotta-go" absenteeism. She wanted a partnership in marriage, didn't think she could ever have one with him, and wanted out.

Speaking in less animated tones, Joe told me of his shattered dreams. "When I started this adventure I had three goals. I'd have a great marriage, an effective ministry in the real world, and a successful business. Tonight, I feel like I'll be lucky if I can hold on to just one out of three." He described how he felt. "You know the competitive Jeep race they run across the Sahara desert?" he asked. "You know how by the end of the event the windshields are caked with dust, mud, and grime? By the time the winner crosses the line, you can't see into the vehicle and the driver can't see out! That's what my life is like. I've been competing in a polluted environment for so long, whatever spiritual life was in me is covered with a layer of crap so thick, nobody can see it from the outside, and I don't even know if it is there anymore."

"The Corinthian syndrome," I said, nodding in understanding.

"What?" he asked.

I reminded Joe of the church at Corinth. The Corinthian church was strategically but perilously located in a pagan center known for the extravagance of its pleasures and vice. Foreign visitors flocked to what was known internationally as the "morally open city" in search of wealth or pleasure. The city boasted the only amphitheater in Greece as well as numerous theaters, taverns, baths, and shops. One young man captured the spirit of Corinth when he wrote, "I am living as becomes a man of breeding. I have a mistress who is very fair. I have never wronged any man. I drink Chian wine, and in all other respects I contrive to satisfy myself, since my private resources are sufficient for these purposes."

A pluralistic, permissive, religious culture flourished in this licentious environment. A variety of Oriental and Hellenistic cults set up shop with their temples, shrines, and altars. Most famous among them was the temple of Aphrodite. Over one thousand priestesses engaged in cult prostitution at this temple, perched eighteen hundred feet above the city and dedicated to the goddess of love.

It was because of this pagan environment that the apostle Paul reminded the Corinthian church that they were called to be set apart, holy in Christ Jesus (1 Corinthians 1:2). He was urging them to remain pure, to avoid sin without isolating themselves from sinners. Yet in this very church, Paul discovered there was a man living with his stepmother in an incestuous relationship, an immorality shunned even by the sexually liberated Corinthian culture. This was a clear case of a church called to be a candle in the darkness, but snuffed out by the winds of moral compromise. In a sex-saturated culture, not unlike ours, the powers of the culture overwhelmed some of the Corinthian Christians. Called to influence the culture, the culture had influenced the church more.

The Essenes, a group in Paul's time, believed that this kind of story proved why people aspiring to holiness—of necessity and for their own spiritual preservation—should get out of the pagan environment and withdraw into an isolated "separated community." Not Paul. Paul tells the Christians not to associate with this morally lapsed *brother*, but he goes on to tell them explicitly that he is *not* telling them to avoid the immoral *unbelievers* of this world, because that would mean getting out of the world completely.

Joe's story illustrates that our journey into the world is a dangerous one. Even though he was intentional in his desire to build a beachhead for the kingdom of God in the advertising world, Joe succumbed to the Corinthian syndrome, and his efforts were not only neutralized but completely destroyed. His instincts to go into the world were proper because to *not go* into the world is explicit disobedience, but his execution was fatally flawed. Now his only choice was to confess his absolute failure, turn from his wicked ways, return governance of his life to God, and allow God to begin the slow process of directing the repair of every damaged aspect of his life.

The Corinthian syndrome can so frighten us that we would like to abandon our calling to go into the world. We need to be reminded about God's protective powers. Read on.

CHAPTER 9

SEEK PROTECTION

TEMPTATIONS COME IN A VARIETY OF forms: workaholism, substance abuse, financial impropriety, and sexual immorality, to name a few. In every case, if you yield to them, you will diminish your effectiveness in taking Jesus into the world. It has been so since the beginning of the church. Way back in the first century, Demas, one of the apostle Paul's protégés, loved the present world and deserted his mentor to live in the prosperous port city of Thessalonica.

Every disciple who follows Jesus into the world will be tempted by the desires of the flesh, the desire of the eyes, the pride in riches. Virtually everyone who intentionally goes into the world intending to be a presence for the gospel places himself or herself in harm's way. So what guards and protects us in such circumstances?

PRAYER

In one of his last prayers on earth, Jesus acknowledged his concern for the disciples as they headed out into the world. He prayed to his Father, "I am not asking you to take them out of the world, but I ask you to protect them from the evil one" (John 17:15). Months earlier he taught his disciples another short prayer, encouraging them to pray it daily: "Lead us not into temptation, but deliver us from the evil one" (Matthew 6:13 NIV). Jesus himself rose up a great while before the day, spending time with his heavenly Father, being equipped for the opportunities, tests, and temptations he would face that day as he headed into the world.

THE HOLY SPIRIT

Jesus promised that after returning to the Father, God would send us an advocate, the Holy Spirit, whose purpose would be to glorify Jesus and act vigorously on our behalf. The Holy Spirit is present with Jesus' disciples each day, available to teach you everything, to remind you of all Jesus said, to give you the very words to say when you get in tight situations. Each day, before going into the world, you should invite the Holy Spirit to take up full residency in your life. God's Spirit is holy and cannot abide sin. Each day as you invite the Holy Spirit to fill you, you are nurturing God's presence in a way that actually repels evil. Jesus was so full of God's presence that the evil spirits would cry out simply because Jesus was in the vicinity.

FEAR OF THE EVIL ONE

After Gordon MacDonald publicly confessed and repented of his marital infidelity, people wondered how it could have ever happened. He compared his vulnerability to Russia whose security was breached when a young East German pilot landed a small plane on Red Square in Moscow. You may recall everyone's amazement that a young, relatively inexperienced pilot in such a small, ill-equipped plane could so easily penetrate Russia's air space, secured as it was by sophisticated detection systems. The pilot's explanation was simple. He flew in low, under the radar. Gordon and each of us familiar with deep failure are aware of the resourcefulness of the Evil One, craftily flying in under our radar, into unprotected areas of our lives. Such fear puts us on alert and makes us aware of our vulnerabilities.

SCARS TO REMIND US OF OUR FAILURES

Once, while mowing the lawn, I tried to negotiate my way under a low-hanging palm tree. The sharp edges of the branch caught my arm, tearing me across the veins on the inside bend of my arm. That was when I was a teenager, and there is still a scar there today. Just last weekend, while teaching my daughters how to use a power mower, I told the story of the scar to warn them of the risks involved in the task they were undertaking.

In the same way our spiritual failures leave scars long after we've been forgiven. Their purpose is to protect us from evil by reminding us of the pain of sin. Joe, who gave in to the Corinthian syndrome, once forgiven, might be less likely to fall again because he has felt the pain of his sin and bears the scars.

THE WORDS AND WEAPONS FROM GOD

When led into the desert and tempted, Jesus quoted the words of God to the Evil One, and the Devil was turned away by the force of Jesus' words. In the battle of dark and light, there are great weapons available against the dark side, and one of them is God's Word. God's words are variously described as food, light for the path, and as a protective and discerning sword against the cosmic powers of this present darkness. Other elements in our protective armor include truth, righteousness, the gospel of peace, faith, and salvation (Ephesians 6:10–17).

The apostle Paul indicates that the proper use of these spiritual weapons requires training. None of us would expect to enter athletic competition or the Olympic arena without discipline and practice, yet for some reason we believe we can enter cosmic spiritual warfare against the Evil One with nary a jog around the block! We train for spiritual warfare by practicing the daily disciplines of prayer, meditating on the words of God, and quieting ourselves so we can listen for the voice of God.

HELP FROM FRIENDS

Jesus expects his disciples to become a close-knit community. None of us should individualistically head into the world as "lone rangers" for God, untethered from the nurture, support, and accountability of our fellow disciples. Men's accountability groups became popular as an outgrowth of Promise Keepers. While not everyone finds these groups helpful, I can tell you this from my own experience: Take a few honest guys who are willing to talk about their darkest deeds and desires, get them probing each other about their actual thoughts and behavior, and it can be a powerful incentive to not sin. I noticed Michael Card, recording artist and Bible teacher, wearing a beeper last time he was in my radio studio and asked him why. He explained that his accountability group was beeper equipped so that in a moment of weakness or crisis, any of the other guys could immediately put out an electronic cry for help.

I was reminded of one of my friends who, years before accountability groups were popular, called me late one night saying he needed help. He had gone to a party that got out of hand, for the first time in his life got drunk, passed out, and now found himself in an upstairs bedroom in a strange house. When he came to, people were still partying hard. His first reaction was not shame, though that came later. His first reaction was fear. How in the world did I get into this awful situation, and how do I get out? He remembered he carried my phone number in his wallet so he called. The familiar voice of a Christian friend was the dose of reality he needed to do the right thing.

A REASSURANCE

I tremble when encouraging Christians to go into the world as a presence for Jesus, because I know we are weak and prone to wander, and we face an adversary who is clever, strategic, and intends to do harm to our mortal souls. And more than ever the world is truly a more dangerous place for our kids and us. But I also know Jesus calls us into the rough and tumble of the world and promises he is more powerful than the Evil One seeking to destroy us. And I am reassured that Jesus sends us out with this prayer for disciples including us:

> I am not asking you to take them out of the world, but I ask you to protect them from the evil one. They do not belong to the world, just as I do not belong to the world. Sanctify them in the truth; your word is truth. As you have sent me into the world, so I have sent them into the world. And for their sakes I sanctify myself, so that they also may be sanctified in truth. I ask not only on behalf of these, but also on behalf of those who will believe in me through their word. (John 17:15–20)

CHAPTER 10

EXPERIENCE THE GOSPEL

RECENTLY MCDONALD'S ASKED THEIR ad agency to conduct a top-secret, six-month study to identify the essential reasons for their success. They felt they needed to regain some focus. In a revelation that made housewives all across America smack their foreheads and say, "Well, duh," McDonald's discovered what consumers expect from them. Are you ready? Here are their shocking findings: quality food; fast, friendly service; good value; and cleanliness. McDonald's referred to this as their "brand essence," and confessed they had strayed at times from the essentials of their brand.

What does this have to do with the gospel? I think it is easy for us to forget what is essential and truly exciting about the gospel and in so doing lose our enthusiasm for personally enjoying the full benefits of the gospel and sharing them with others. When I listen to the cries of the human heart I am reminded of the ways in which the gospel is tailor-made to satisfy our deepest human yearnings and needs.

OUR LONGING FOR GOD

We long for a personal and intimate relationship with the transcendent God. This internal longing for God drives us to seek Him. It is the sojourn the character Ernest Hemingway gives voice to in the last lines of John deGroot's one-man drama, *Papa*.

> Close by the very summit of Kilimanjaro, almost to the very top, lies the frozen body of a great male leopard. And what drove this proud creature alone to those fatal heights? And what made him go there? Climb that high? Some people believe he'd been badly wounded and was trying to run from his pain. But the natives say, he was seeking his God.

During a recent interview with National Book Award winner Robert Stone, I mentioned reading that when he abandoned the Catholicism of his youth he felt liberated, only to wake up twenty years later feeling like "half his head was missing." He replied, "I think it happens to a lot of people. You leave religion with a tremendous sense of liberation and then years later you discover that something really important is missing . . . and you either start all over again and go back and try to reclaim it, or else you substitute something else for it." He went on to say, "There is that element of man as Pascal said, 'The world everywhere gives evidence of a vanished God and man in all his actions gives evidence of a longing for that God.' So you make do in small ways. One way or other you've got to fill that space somehow."

This yearning for the transcendent God is universal, experienced by young and old. Douglas Coupland, the quintessential Generation Xer, reveals his own hunger for God in the book *Life After God*. He describes being raised in a culturally relativistic environment without any religious instruction. Near the end of the book he drops his bombshell.

> Now here is my secret. I tell it to you with an openness of heart that I doubt I shall ever achieve again, so I pray that you are in a quiet room as you hear these words. My secret is that I need God—I am sick and can no longer make it alone. I need God to help me give, because I no longer seem capable of giving; to help me be kind, as I no longer seem capable of kindness; to help me love, as I seem beyond able to love.

OUR LONGING FOR IDENTITY AND PURPOSE

We long to understand our personal identity and purpose. British social philosopher Charles Handy says, "Ours is an age of the Hungry Spirit in which man is on a quest for purpose in the modern world." In 1997 researcher George Barna reported that 43 percent of adults are trying to figure out the meaning and purpose of life. Why are we here? What is our purpose? What is the meaning of my life? These are the questions most humans ask quietly, privately, and often desperately.

OUR LONGING FOR COMMUNITY

We long for a sense of community. I recall a conversation with Barry Lopez, another winner of the National Book Award. In the introduction to *About This Life: Journeys on the Threshold of Memory*, he says, "I believe in all human societies there is a desire to love and be loved, to experience the full fierceness of human emotion, and to make a measure of the sacred part of one's life." Intrigued by this comment, we engaged in an off-the-air discussion of his spiritual journey and its connection to community.

Lopez told me about a recent writer's conference he'd attended. Some imaginative soul pulled together a group of novelists for a private, by-invitation retreat with other successful authors. By nature loners, most authors attended only out of curiosity and feelings of obligation to their publishers, mixed with some vague fears of retribution. By the end of the first afternoon the discussion turned to a simple question: Is there a common theme in our writing? Is there a preoccupation we share as we explore life at the end of the twentieth century? Interestingly this widely diverse group of independent individualists found one point of unanimous agreement. They concluded, "The one theme all our work shares is a universal human longing for community."

Sociologist Robert Wuthnow agrees, saying in *I Came Away Stronger*, "America at the end of the twentieth century is fundamentally a society in transition. It is far from clear what kind of society we will have in the next century. One thing is clear, the search for community and for the sacred will continue to characterize the American people."

OUR LONGING FOR FORGIVENESS

We long for release from guilt and shame. In the film *Grand Canyon*, Danny Glover, playing the role of a tow-truck driver, summarizes the human dilemma in his message to a young gang leader. An attorney, played by Kevin Kline, is on his way home from a Laker's game when he takes a wrong exit, gets lost, and ends up with car trouble in the bad part of town. He calls a tow truck, but before it arrives, a local gang moves slowly and menacingly toward Kline's car. Just in time, tow-truck driver Danny Glover arrives to intervene. He takes the leader of the gang aside and says,

Man, the world ain't supposed to work like this. Maybe you don't know that, but this ain't the way it's supposed to be. I'm supposed to be able to do my job without askin' you if I can. And that dude is supposed to be able to wait with his car without you rippin' him off. Everything's supposed to be different than what it is here.

A *Wall Street Journal* editorial in December 1991 put it this way. "The U.S. has a drug problem and a high school sex problem and a welfare problem and an AIDS problem and a rape problem. None of this will go away until more people in positions of responsibility are willing to come forward and explain, in frankly moral terms, that some of the things people do nowadays are wrong."

Despite persistent attempts to rationalize away the concept of sin through relativistic exercises in values clarification, all humans recognize there are right and wrong actions. We experience guilty feelings when we do something wrong. In addition to feeling guilty for what we have done, psychologists also tell us our feelings of shame are rooted, not in what we have done, but in feelings of inadequacy about *who we are*.

Our Longing for Eternity

We long to understand our eternal destiny. *People* magazine reported the moving story of Beach Boy Carl Wilson's memorial service. At the funeral Carl's brother Brian fell into his wife's arms and cried out, "Carl's gone. He's gone, and I don't know where he went." In that moment Brian Wilson gave voice to life's universal question: what happens when we die?

The overall impact of these unfulfilled human longings is a general lack of well-being. Psychologists sometimes refer to this as "free-floating anxiety." Writer John Updike summarized it saying, "We may live well, but that cannot cease the suspicion that we no longer live nobly."

SATISFYING OUR LONGINGS

How do we satisfy these universal human longings? How can we restore a feeling of well-being? Joni Mitchell comes uncannily close to the correct answer in her song "Woodstock," where she cries, "We've got to get ourselves back to the garden."

There is within every human a vestigial awareness of a time when all things were right. It is a distant, ancient reminiscence of the Garden of Eden. Imbedded in our collective memory is this intuitive knowledge and vague awareness of a place and time where we experienced a personal relationship with the transcendent God, understood our identity and purpose, enjoyed a sense of community, knew no guilt or shame, and were confident of our eternal destiny. We were blessed by God (Genesis 1:28). In the Bible "to be blessed" refers to the well-being that comes as God's gift to humans.

And then came sin.

In an age when we don't often talk about the "s" word, it is extremely important to understand what sin really is. Oswald Chambers clarifies this in *My Utmost for His Highest*, saying, "The nature of sin is not immorality and wrongdoing, but the nature of self-realization, which leads us to say, 'I am my own God.'" When the first humans displaced God with themselves, they, along with their future offspring, were expelled from the garden of well-being. We lost our personal relationship with God. Gone was our assurance of meaning and identity, our unity and equality of relationship was shattered, our eternal destiny was displaced with death. Since that time all humans have longed for what was ours in the garden.

And then came the gospel.

The good news is that God is repairing all that unraveled when humans were expelled from the garden. As a result, we can again experience the well-being that comes with being blessed by God. All this is available through Jesus, God's only Son.

Through Jesus' life and teaching we learn that God has established a new kingdom providing access to God in a relationship so personal, accessible, and intimate that we can call God "Daddy" ("Abba" in the Lord's prayer). In God's new kingdom, relationships are built on a covenant of love and forgiveness. There is an equality in this kingdom because there is "no longer Jew or Greek, there is no longer slave or free, there is no longer male and female; for all of you are one in Christ Jesus" (Galatians 3:28). In this kingdom we again embrace our identity as those uniquely created in God's image, designed to express our talents cooperatively with others in work that glorifies God and blesses others.

Furthermore, through his death and resurrection Jesus offers freedom from sin and guilt. In his death Jesus pays the debt for our sin, relieving us of our guilt. In his resurrection he demonstrates his power to offer a new and transformed human nature free from shame and destined for eternity with God.

All of this is ours because of God the Father's great love. In the familiar story of the Prodigal Son, Jesus tells the universal human story of a son leaving his father, realizing the error of his ways (sin), and returning home. His father, whose love had never diminished, sees his son at a distance, runs to meet him, hugs him, and throws a celebratory party. The *New York Times,* in reviewing Ron Hansen's *Atticus,* caught this spirit and concluded, "This is the story of a son behaving absolutely unforgivably; and his father forgiving him absolutely." God loves us extravagantly, is willing to forgive our ancestral and personal rebellion, and wants to restore our well-being. *This is good news indeed!*

So how should we respond to such a gospel?

RECEIVE THE GOSPEL

The seeker needs to receive God's gift by following Jesus. As we've seen, the gospel addresses the essential longings of the human soul. The gospel announces Jesus Christ as the restorer of our souls and the way back to the garden. And the gospel invites seekers to repent of their sins, deny self, take up a cross, and follow Jesus, trusting in him for a new, abundant, and eternal life.

EXPERIENCE THE GOSPEL

The believer needs to experience and enjoy the gospel each day. This reminder of the gospel's essence is also a call for Christians to celebrate what God provided in this great gospel. Just as McDonald's forgot the essentials of their success, many Christians forget or take the gospel for granted. I once asked Claude King, coauthor of the Bible study *Experiencing God*, to explain the runaway success of what is really a very elemental course. He replied, "Western Christianity is often so propositional and didactic that it has reduced God to a series of intellectual premises to be believed, or attributes to be learned, but not actually experienced!"

The gospel is more than a set of ideas to be believed; it is a personal and restorative relationship with God who desires to bless us each day with well-being, identity, purpose, community, release from our guilt and shame, and the assurance of eternal life with God.

Why are so many of us "don't ask, don't tell" Christians? I fear it is because we sometimes lose our wonder and appreciation for the essential gospel. Effectively sharing the gospel with other people starts with experiencing the restorative power of the gospel each day. Being attentive to the gospel in our own life is the prelude to sharing it with others. Joseph Campbell once told Bill Moyers in a PBS interview, "We serve the world by being spiritually well." The late Henri Nouwen said in *Sabbatical Journey*, "The first question [for the disciple] is not: 'How much do I do?' or how many people do I help out, but 'am I interiorly at peace?'"

If you want to take Jesus into your world, attend to your soul in relationship with the living and loving God. And enjoy all the benefits of this great gospel!

■ LIVE THE GOSPEL

There is a life-changing, transforming power in God's presence. After Jesus' ascension, that power was personalized in the gift of the Holy Spirit who indwells each individual believer. The Holy Spirit changed Peter from a betrayer to a bold apostle. The Holy Spirit so completely imprinted the powerful presence of Jesus on the church in Antioch, that for the first time onlookers coined the term *Christian*, which meant "the Christ folk."

When you allow the Holy Spirit to transform you, you will take Jesus more effectively into your world.

Since the gospel is more than a set of ideas to be believed, but is in fact a restorative relationship with God, this restoration process should be observable in your life. As legendary coach John Wooden said, "If I were ever prosecuted for my religion, I truly hope there would be enough evidence to convict."

Saint Francis once said, "Preach the gospel, and if you must use words." He's in good company. H. M. Stanley discovered David Livingston in Central Africa. After having spent time with him, he said, "If I had been with him any longer I would have been compelled to be a Christian, and he never spoke to me about it at all."

This follows the pattern revealed by the apostle Peter who said, "Conduct yourself honorably among the Gentiles, so that, though they malign you as evildoers, they may see your honorable deeds and glorify God when he comes to judge" (1 Peter 2:12). Peter taught that a wife's exemplary life could prompt her husband to be won without a word, and observers would ask for the reason for the hope so in evidence in a disciple's life.

In his classic ancient Greek work on rhetoric, Aristotle said there are three components in persuasion: logic (*logos*), passion (*pathos*), and integrity (*ethos*). He believed that all the logic and passion in the world would not persuade a person who could observe that your life didn't match your words. Only when you state your case reasonably, passionately, *and with integrity* will it carry great weight.

I am reminded of a famous story of Gandhi who, when making his first trip to England in 1930, disembarked in Southhampton and while still on the gangway was overwhelmed by journalists asking questions. One of them asked, "Mr. Gandhi, what do you think of Western civilization?" Mr. Gandhi replied, "I think it would be a good idea." Today many people have heard of Jesus, but think Christianity is only an idea or set of beliefs because they have never seen it in action. Yet the single most credible argument on behalf of Christianity is its demonstration in the life of an individual follower of Jesus.

So how will people see the gospel in your life?

They Will Observe Your Devotion to God

The Westminster Confession summarizes our essential purpose this way: "What is the chief end of man? Man's chief end is to glorify God, and to enjoy him forever." J. S. Bach clearly understood this, saying, "Music's only purpose should be for the glory of God and the recreation of the human spirit." Bach routinely initialed the letters S.D.G. (Soli Deo Gloria) at the end of each manuscript, indicating that all his work was intended as a reflection of God's glory. The late Mother Teresa said her purpose was "to do, to make, to be something beautiful for God." Another time she said she was "a pencil in God's hands."

Recall the memorable line in *Chariots of Fire* when Eric Liddell balances a call to serve God in China with a concurrent call to run fast. Explaining this to his missions-obsessed sister he says, "God has called me to be a missionary in China, and I will go. But he has also called me to run fast, and when I run I feel God's pleasure." Liddell's career decisions were not based on money, security, or even the prestige of running the Olympics. Liddell was determined to obey and bring glory to God in all he did.

This devotion is particularly powerful when people see our devotion to God even in hard times. My own faith has been strengthened through the witness of our teenage daughter, Jessica, who has suffered chronic migraines since she was nine years old, yet whose love for and commitment to God is deep and unwavering and whose joyful spirit is contagious.

They Will Observe Your Awe for Our Powerful and Transcendent God

In *Your God Is Too Small,* J. B. Phillips urges Christians not to settle for a God made in our own image, but rather to seek the one true God. Donald McCullough updated this theme in his superb book *The Trivialization of God,* observing, "Visit an average congregation on a Sunday morning and you will likely find a congregation comfortably relating to a deity who fits nicely within precise doctrinal positions, or who lends almighty support to social crusades, or who conforms to individual experiences. But you will not likely find much awe." He goes on to quote Annie Dillard, who describes today's Christians as "cheerful, brainless tourists on a packaged tour of the Absolute."

In *Teaching a Stone to Talk*, Annie Dillard adds, "On the whole I do not find Christians, outside the catacombs, sufficiently sensible of the conditions. Does anybody have the foggiest idea what sort of power we so blithely invoke? Or, as I suspect, does no one believe a word of it? The churches are children playing on the floor with their chemistry sets, mixing up a batch of TNT to kill a Sunday morning. It is madness to wear ladies' straw hats and velvet hats to church; we should all be wearing crash helmets. Ushers should issue life preservers and signal flares; they should lash us to our pews. For the sleeping god may draw us out to where we can never return."

Your intense devotion and authentic encounter with the transcendent God will attract people to the gospel, offering those who seek it a relationship with the living and transcendent God. I am a disciple today because I watched people who indisputably knew God and by example helped me believe I could experience God too. I remember as a ten-year-old listening to my grandfather read the Bible to us each morning after breakfast at his cabin in the redwoods. I can't explain how, but I knew Grandpa was taking us into the presence of an all-powerful God, who was in the room with us, because we were in the room with our grandfather who knew God. Grandpa was dedicated to a radical life of complete devotion to an unmanageable God who regularly led him out of his comfort zones. He showed me the way by his example.

They Will Observe You Living a Life That Blesses and Serves Other People

Frederick Buechner said in *Wishful Thinking*, "The place God calls you to is the place where your deep gladness and the world's deep hunger meet." Christians are called to occupy and serve in places of deep need in society, just as Jesus did.

When I interviewed Sri Lankan Vinoth Ramachandra, author of *Gods That Fail*, he quoted George Steiner who said, "We live in an age when God's presence is no longer held to be tenable and God's absence isn't felt as loss." I asked Vinoth how we could prove God as "tenable and present" to such a person. He replied, "Such a person must see God in the lives of Jesus' followers." He reminded me that Christianity first gained a foothold in Sri Lanka because, "In Sri Lanka Christians were in the forefront of developing the medical system and delivered health care in the name of Jesus." People never forgot.

Unfortunately people do not always see our gospel lived out. In *One-Sided Christianity*, Ron Sider tells the story of a Jewish university student in South Africa who decided, "I do not want to be like these white Christians here. They sing about the love of Jesus. But they don't care about justice in South Africa." In *The Jesus I Never Knew*, Philip Yancey tells the story of a Chicago prostitute unable to buy food for her two-year-old daughter. When her friend asked if she had ever thought of going to a church for help, she cried, "Church! Why would I ever go there? I was already feeling terrible about myself. They'd just make me feel worse!"

Despite the obvious and oft-reported failures of Christians to show the gospel, every day millions of people are the recipients of random acts of kindness and sacrificial service delivered by Christians who love God and live out the gospel by showing love in practical ways. I see the spirit of servanthood in Anne and Wayne Gordon, who upon graduation from college turned away from suburban comforts to move into Chicago's Lawndale neighborhood among the nation's poorest to begin the Lawndale Community Church, a wonderful model for urban ministry. Millions of Jesus' disciples are present as "salt and light" throughout the world, just as Jesus said they would be. Their acts of love are a compelling testimony to people who wonder if Jesus is real.

Closer to home, my own attraction to serving others was shaped by watching my parents give of themselves sacrificially and behind the scenes in the churches they served. Both of my parents are extremely talented communicators, but their truest eloquence was in daily and selfless service to my handicapped brother, who needed constant care and affection. This validated my father's preaching and my mother's teaching and made the gospel tangible and real to me as an impressionable kid.

THEY WILL OBSERVE YOUR CARING COMMUNITY

In *Sabbatical Journey*, we read about Henri Nouwen's one-year leave of absence from his life of intense community at L'Arche Daybreak. Nouwen, who longed for communion and intimacy all his life, had finally found it in community with the physically and intellectually disabled. Ironically, given a year to do as he pleased, Nouwen planned a year away from community to focus his energies on prayer and writing, both of which require a solitude difficult to attain at a place like L'Arche.

In what turned out to be the final year of his life, Nouwen discovered he was drawn irrepressibly to relationships and people. His sabbatical schedule was a whirlwind of visits, trips, and speaking engagements. Nouwen craved time with other people so earnestly that though he could have enjoyed solitude in private hotel rooms he often made arrangements to stay in homes with friends. Instead of driving alone Nouwen usually drove with someone else, or took a bus. His everyday life was connected to people and rooted in the close relationships he had nurtured throughout his life. Sue Mosteller, his dear friend and editor, wrote:

> After nine years at L' Arche the community sent him off with a mandate to say no to all work except writing. We overlooked, however, his need and gift for friendship and what his appropriate response to that might be. *Sabbatical* recounts an "odyssey" of friendship; it requires the stature of a "Ulysses" to make the exhausting journey and write five books along the way. Henri meets, celebrates, consoles, counsels, and connects with *over a thousand people, and in friendship he mentions over six hundred of them by name.*

Reflecting on the difference between his plans for a year of solitude and the reality of one of the busiest relational seasons of his life, Nouwen explained the difference by saying, "God must remain the God of surprises." But he also realized that community now played a central role in his life. "Community is so much more than living and working together. It is a bond of the heart that has no physical limitations. Indeed it is candles burning in different places of the world, all praying the same silent prayer of friendship and love." His journal entry the day after Christmas reflects the intensity of his passion for friendship and community.

> This afternoon I wrote many postcards. While writing I experienced a deep love for all the friends I was writing to. My heart was full of gratitude and affection, and I wished I could embrace each of my friends and let them know how much they mean to me and how much I miss them. It seems that sometimes distance creates closeness, absence creates presence, and loneliness creates community! I felt my whole being, body mind and spirit, yearning to give and receive love without condition, without fear, without reservation.

This life in loving community is longed for in today's society and when in evidence will not go unobserved. People today will be attracted to the gospel when they see what pagans saw in the first post-ascension gathering of believers. They loved one another, honored one another, esteemed one another, were likeminded with one another, forbore one another, were kind and tenderhearted toward one another, submitted to one another, admonished one another, abounded in love one toward another, comforted one another, edified one another, confessed faults to one another, bore no grudge toward one another, showed compassion for one another, were hospitable to one another, greeted one another with a kiss, ministered to one another, and so on.

G. K. Chesterton once said, "The Christian ideal has not been tried and found wanting. It has been found difficult and not tried." Living the gospel consistently in real life is difficult, and none of us is perfect. But it's better to aspire to living the gospel and fail, experiencing and giving witness to God's wonderful grace and forgiveness in the process, than to settle for mediocrity. When the gospel is lived out in an individual, warts and all, it makes a huge difference. Witness the impact of the very public and self-confessed imperfect Christian, Billy Graham.

After a story about Billy Graham in *U.S. News and World Report*, a letter to the editor illustrated the importance of one disciple living out the gospel. Keith Beutler wrote, "Many people will disagree with the Rev. Billy Graham's beliefs, but who can argue against his life? It is a testament of sorts in its own right. Anyone who was so pivotal a player in late-twentieth century society, yet has maintained integrity, deserves to be heard."

Amen and amen. Live out the gospel, and taking Jesus effectively into the world will follow!

CHAPTER 12

▪ SEE

SIXTH SENSE WAS A BOX OFFICE SUR-
prise, garnering over 250 million
dollars in revenue. Much of the
box office success is due to return
visits from people who had to
watch it a second time to figure
out why they missed something
obvious the first time around. The
film's surprise ending succeeds,
because most people base their
view of reality on what they see,
while this film requires you to
focus on what you aren't seeing
though it is clearly there.

In a similar way, I've come to realize that God is at work all around me, but often I don't see it.

LIKE THE BLIND MAN

Yesterday I saw something I never noticed in a familiar Bible story. I hate it when that happens! In my Bible the story in Luke 18:35 is titled, "A Blind Beggar Receives His Sight." You probably know the story.

Jesus is approaching Jericho when he passes a blind man sitting by the roadside begging. When he learns Jesus is nearby, the blind man yells, "Jesus, Son of David, have mercy on me." Irritated at the blind man's yelling, the crowd sternly orders him to be quiet. He persists in crying out for mercy. Finally, Jesus stops and asks what he can do for the blind man. "My teacher, let me see again" was the simple reply (Mark 10:51). Jesus said, "Go; your faith has made you well" (Mark 10:52). Immediately the blind man received his sight and followed Jesus, glorifying God.

Here's the part I never saw before. This isn't just a story about a blind man. It is a story about a blind crowd! Remember the irritated crowd who tried to quiet the blind man? After the blind man is healed we read, "All the people, when they saw it, praised God" (Luke 18:43). I never before noticed the phrase "all the people, when they saw it." In an exquisite little literary twist we are reminded that it isn't just the blind man who can't see; the crowd is blind as well! Until the blind man's sight is restored, the crowd has not seen Jesus clearly. Like the crowd, we are in Jesus' presence every day but are often inattentive and don't see it!

FOCUSING ON THE WRONG THINGS

I remember one of my birding outings with our daughter Heidi who was about eleven at the time. Up at 6 A.M., we headed into the woods near our home. By 6:15 we'd already seen robins, cardinals, goldfinch, and killdeer, but I was ready to branch off the meadow and head into the woods angling toward the river. I like to follow the narrow deer trails. I call this adventure. My kids call it getting lost. Due to recent rainstorms, that day you could also call it getting really, really muddy. Heidi was wearing some pretty nice khakis, and because the trail was intermittently either submerged under water or was a nice sloshy mix of mud, her khakis were now a lovely mud brown. I warned Heidi to roll up her pants, but she was too busy swatting off mosquitoes and grabbing branches to avoid being sucked underwater in the ever-deepening puddles. It was a grim situation. In moments like this a man can hear a voice in his head. It is a woman's voice. It is his wife's voice. It is not a happy voice. You hear in the tone of her voice that you are going to die when you get home.

Just then we heard what sounded like a helicopter not more than three feet above our heads. It was a huge barn owl leaving the branch just above us and spreading its wings to full span to reach the other side of the river. In focusing on the muddy trail, we had completely missed the owl that was literally right before our eyes on a branch arched over the path. Not only that, we actually hadn't seen the river, which was only five feet to the west of the trail!

Just as we don't see things in the physical world, we are often blind spiritually. Every day, God is at work around us and we miss it because we are focusing on the wrong things.

God Is at Work

In Henry Blackaby and Claude King's study series, *Experiencing God,* the very first principle is—God is always at work around you. But here is the problem. God is at work around us, but we don't see it because we aren't looking for it. Blackaby tells of his church's desire to minister to students at a nearby college campus. One Sunday he pulled the students in church together and challenged them to keep their eyes open for God working on campus, so they could join God in what He was doing. He read them John 6:44, "No one can come to me [Jesus] unless the Father who sent me draws him" and explained that no one will seek God unless God is already at work in their lives. "When you see someone seeking God or asking about spiritual matters, you are seeing God at work," he explained.

The next Wednesday one of the girls, Kathy, reported an encounter with a girl with whom she'd had classes for two years. The girl wanted to talk, and instead of going to their next class Kathy and the girl went to the cafeteria to talk. As a result of this one conversation, three Bible studies were started in the girl's dorm and two in the men's dorm. But it all started because Kathy was attentive to the "God possibilities" and decided to talk to the girl instead of going to class.

A Divine Appointment

Like blind men, I believe we miss these divine appointments almost every day. It happened to me during a period of time when my wife, Kathy, and I were in a small group studying *Experiencing God*.

I was leading a group on a tour of Israel. My wife's mother Pat was so excited that Kathy would be going on the trip, she decided to come along and invited her other daughter Tricia and my brother-in-law Bob to take the trip as well. This of course provided opportunities for mother-in-law jokes. Some people were getting skittish about taking the trip because there had been some isolated incidents of violence in Israel. I would say, "My mother-in-law is going to be on the bus with me, and this assures it will be more dangerous on the bus than outside." People would laugh, Pat would groan—life is good!

A few weeks before we were to leave, Kathy told me of a conversation she'd had with Bob in which he sensed that this trip would be a spiritual experience for him. At the time Bob and Tricia were not attending church, and in fact they had attended only sporadically since getting married ten years ago. We dutifully reported this to our *Experiencing God* group and asked for prayer.

On the night we were to leave for Israel, we were sitting at La Guardia airport waiting for the flight. Bob and I were talking about silly stuff (my specialty) when he asked a question out of the blue. "Dick, I know you were on a church staff once. Can you baptize people?"

Thinking this was a random request for information I said that technically I could and deftly turned the subject to silly stuff. I could write an episode of Veggie Tales. For goodness sakes, *I am an episode of Veggie Tales!*

A few minutes later Bob commented. "I noticed we'll be stopping at the Jordan River and they'll allow people on the tour a chance to be baptized there.

Again, I commented how interesting that was and continued blathering on about nothing. Finally, though, it dawned on me that something was happening here. I slowly turned to Bob and asked, "Are you thinking about getting baptized at the Jordan River?"

Bob smiled and said, "Well, yeah, I was thinking about it."

Then I muddled on. "Were you wanting to know if I could be the one who baptizes you?"

A look of relief came over his face, and he said, "I was thinking that would be really cool!"

I was speechless. Here God was answering our prayer about Bob, and I, an advanced student of *Experiencing God*, just about missed point number one: God is always at work around you! A week later I baptized Bob and Tricia in the Jordan River. Life *really is good!*

People around us are on a spiritual journey. They are like blind men trying to find their way. Sometimes their agony is so great, it is as if they are crying out for mercy. God is at work in their lives directing them into our path. But we are so often focused on the mud we miss the people in our path. Like the old poem says, "Two men looked out from prison bars, one saw mud, the other saw stars."

The moral of the story? Keep your eyes open to what God is doing around you.

CHAPTER 13

■ FEEL

I'M A GUY. BY DEFINITION THIS MEANS I am clueless about feelings.

I'm an American. This means I've witnessed tears flowing and emotions running high on television talk shows, where modern-day priests, like Jerry Springer, Montel Williams, and Oprah Winfrey alternatingly provoke, forgive, and condemn folks who seem normal until you hear their wacky revelations in the public confessional of daytime television.

I'm a Christian. This means I saw Jim and Tammy Bakker go

down in flames. I watched Jimmy Swaggart weep uncontrollably as he confessed his wrongdoing. I've heard about snake handlers' frenzied dancing in the South and people barking like dogs and roaring like lions in a Toronto church near the airport. All this is done in the name of Jesus.

What's an observant, American, Christian, clueless guy to do about feelings?

Because Jesus was a man and I am committed to following in his footsteps, it seems reasonable to learn from him. Even a cursory reading of the gospels reveals that Jesus experienced emotions, wept, and channeled his emotions in compassion toward other people. Evidently feelings have their proper place in the Christian life.

Jesus Experienced Feelings

Jesus, the Messiah, is described by Isaiah as "a man of sorrows and acquainted with grief" (Isaiah 53:3). He allowed his pain to form tears that rolled down his cheeks. Jesus wept for Jerusalem when he realized the hardship people would experience for failing to see the "visitation of God" (Luke 19:41). At Lazarus's grave, he was "greatly disturbed in spirit and deeply moved" (John 11:35). He experienced emotional trauma universally associated with a symbol of suffering, the cross. On the cross he experienced the *loneliness* of being forsaken, endured *shame*, and was sustained by the *joy* that was set before him (Hebrews 12:2).

Jesus Felt Compassion

Jesus' sorrow moved him into the muddle of people's pain. When expansive crowds of dirty, sweaty, diseased, despised, forsaken villagers thronged to meet him, Jesus was "moved with compassion" because these bedraggled, confused, marginalized men and women were harassed and helpless like lost sheep without a shepherd (Matthew 9:36). When the hungry crowd longed for food (Matthew 15:32), when the lame hobbled toward him for healing (Matthew 14:14), when two blind men begged for their sight (Matthew 20:32)—in each of these cases Jesus took action, not just to verify his Messiahship, but because he felt a deep compassion that moved him to action.

What drew people to Jesus and persuaded them to deny themselves and follow him? Was it his authoritative teaching or his miracles and healing? Was it Jesus' compassion and caring? Was it some combination of all of them?

As I mentioned in an earlier chapter, in his classic book on rhetoric, Aristotle said feelings are an essential element in persuasion. In addition to a logical argument (*logos*), backed up by personal integrity (*ethos*), Aristotle believed the effective communicator should display authentic feelings (*pathos*). Thus the phrase, "They'll never care how much you know until they know how much you care" originates in one of history's greatest rhetoricians and was validated in the life of Jesus. Jesus' teaching was compelling because his words were authenticated by his life. He exhibited love and compassion.

Uncaring Christians

When homosexual Matthew Shepherd was beaten to death in Wyoming, family and friends attended his funeral. Unfortunately, Fred Phelps and a few others were also there, carrying signs that said things like "God hates fags." They claimed to be there in the name of Jesus. It made me sick. It is clear that people like Phelps do not represent Jesus, because love and compassion mark an authentic representation of Jesus.

It seems easy to discern that Fred Phelps lacks compassion, but is it possible that in God's sight we also lack compassion in a subtle but equally unacceptable form? In our pursuit of the American Dream, have we turned our back on the poor? In our disgust with the "don't blame me mentality" have we become deaf to the cry for help behind the excuses? In our fighting a culture war, has our pro-life conviction made us uncaring for the woman choosing an abortion? Are we entertained rather than hurt and moved by the parade of messed-up people on the daily television talk shows? Do we join our neighbors in gossiping about and mocking the weird family down the street? Are we put off by the shabbily dressed, smelly drunk on the park bench? Can we watch news footage of Bosnia or Rwanda and feel nothing?

THE WORLD NEEDS COMPASSION

Last week I heard a Generation Xer tell of his decision to find creative ways to reach his generation with the gospel. It all started with a serious mistake he made two years ago. What was his mistake? He said, "Two years ago I prayed to see my generation through God's eye, and I've been weeping ever since."

In America, though we are wealthy, we suffer from the cumulative and painful effects of breaking God's law. We are swimming in a sea of broken relationships, violence, abuse, and addictive behavior of every kind. While the older generation feels pushed aside, the younger generation sings their suffering like the proverbial canary in the cage.

I recall the reaction to Kurt Cobain's suicide. The night after he died thousands of his peers gathered spontaneously for a candlelight vigil at the International Fountain in Seattle. I was struck by what seemed a sincere outpouring of emotion, so I opened the phone lines on my talk show to see what response it elicited from our audience. Truthfully, I didn't know what to expect. I am an older guy, hosting a show known for getting people to think, so purging feelings was not our daily fare. Surprisingly, calls came out of the woodwork. "It's so sad." "His songs connected with how I feel." "Nobody has touched me so deeply." "I feel like I've lost my best friend."

I remember the first time Tom Beaudoin, author of *Virtual Faith*, told me that suffering is a dominant theme for his peers. I looked at him like he had just dropped from another planet. How do BMW driving, Starbucks coffee drinking, Hilfiger or Abercrombie wearing, cell phone toting, indulged millennials get off describing themselves as a suffering generation? Tom said his generation suffered from feelings of abandonment and disillusionment. They were materially rich but spiritually impoverished.

Donna Gaines describes the same thing in *Teenage Wasteland*, her book about the suicidal angst of kids in upscale Bergen County. After interviewing her I read her comments about Cobain's death in a 1994 *Rolling Stone* magazine article.

> Many kids feel trapped in a cycle of futility and despair. Adults have abandoned an entire generation by failing to provide for or protect them or prepare them for independent living. Yet when young people began to exhibit symptoms of neglect reflected in their rates of suicide, homicide, substance abuse, school failure, recklessness, and general misery, adults condemned them as a group of apathetic, illiterate, amoral losers.

Patricia Hersch, author of *A Tribe Apart*, agrees and says that today's teen listens to Marilyn Manson and Goth groups "as a result of feeling isolated and spiritually lonely."

Recently I was stranded at a hotel between meetings and decided to check out the TV. Montel Williams was doing a show about teenage girls wanting to connect with their mothers. There they sat next to the bewildered mothers with whom they wanted to be reunited. A thirteen-year-old talked about how she felt as she watched her mother gravitate from one abusive relationship to the next. "These guys rant, rave, and hit my mom, and she keeps coming back for more. Meanwhile she has no time for me." Another girl told about moving from relative to relative, because her mother's substance-abuse problem made living with her impossible.

Now straight for six months, the mother lived in a different state and didn't even phone her daughter because "I don't have enough money." When Montel suggested to the mother that she could move closer to her daughter, it seemed this basic thought had never occurred to her. The daughter wept as she described lying awake at night trying to imagine a normal mother-daughter relationship.

I teared up as I thought about the thousands of broken lives, the people all around me who, in the words of the Steve Green song, "need the Lord."

PEOPLE'S PAIN CAN BE A PATHWAY TO GOD

Many people will come to Jesus through the portal of their pain, not through a carefully constructed rational argument. I'm thinking of an incident that happened over twenty years ago. It was 1975 in New England and a major snowstorm was in progress. Being generally of unsound mind, having migrated from California, and therefore, not actually understanding the phrase "travel alert," I was slowly working my way in a no-visibility snowstorm from Massachusetts to New Hampshire. I was scheduled to speak at a family retreat for a regional group of denominational churches.

New Englanders, not being Californians, and instead, being of sound mind and clearly understanding the concept of no-visibility-severe-travel-alerts, possess nowhere within them a genetic or conditioned inclination to risk life and limb traveling in a snowstorm under any circumstances. This being said, they certainly were not about to take such a risk to hear some young Californian and recent seminary graduate speak on any subject, let alone the family, which at his age he would know little about. By late Friday night the combination of blizzard conditions and common sense resulted in a total attendance of a paltry fifteen people at the spacious, snowed-in lodge.

Disappointed by the attendance, but duly earnest, I launched into what was to be a clever exposition and reinterpretation of the time-worn and theologically suspect phrase, "the fatherhood of God and the brotherhood of man." I chose this theme because I was forewarned there might be pagans aboard, so even though the theme was family, they wanted evangelism to kick off the weekend.

As I began unfolding of idea of God as Father, I noticed a striking-looking blonde woman in her thirties starting to weep. Soon her supply of Kleenex was dwindling and my already diminutive audience was about to shrink by one. *What's eating her?* I wondered in all my glorious male obtuseness. It did not occur to me that a hapless pagan had fought through the storm to meet Jesus that night, but later I learned that this is precisely what had happened.

It turns out that Sarah's father had died two weeks earlier. Theirs had been a highly conflicted relationship. As I spoke of God the Father, it triggered a flood of memories of the dashed hopes and recurring disappointments she'd experienced with her earthly father. It also raised more than a few unanswered questions about the character of God as Father. After the retreat, over the next weeks Sarah literally "felt" her way into God's kingdom as she pushed through her earthly sorrow, leading her to repentance and into the arms of her Father-God.

SEVEN OBSTACLES TO SPONTANEOUS COMPASSION

When functioning properly, our heart should spontaneously pump God's compassion into every human encounter every day. So why is compassion so rare even among people who claim to follow Jesus?

1. We've Never Experienced Our Own Pain

Some people cannot be compassionate because they have never allowed themselves to experience and understand their own pain. This is what happened to a friend of mine, whose first appointment with a counselor ended with the counselor's words, "I see a man with an active mind and an empty heart." From childhood, my friend had expended immense amounts of mental energy avoiding emotions he didn't want to deal with. His blockage of emotions about himself made him unable to empathize with others who were in pain.

2. We Love Out of Obligation

Because Jesus commanded us to love one another, some Christians care about other people only to fulfill their obligation to God. While theoretically one might obey Jesus' love commandment without "feeling" anything for the other person, this kind of obligatory love is not what we see in Jesus. Jesus' compassion was not born of mere duty. Jesus *felt* with people. Jesus wept.

3. We're Blind to People's Pain

Compassion requires us to see the pain in other people. Long ago, I was injured in a college basketball game. An opposing player's elbow collided with my face and split the skin under my eye. When the bleeding wouldn't stop, my coach sent me to an emergency room for late-night stitches. The preoccupied ER attendant entered the room and asked which finger I had broken—totally missing the blood gushing under my eye. Someone had told him my finger was broken so that is what he looked for, but even casual observation would have revealed my true condition. We too often miss people's deepest needs.

4. We Are Self-Absorbed

Because compassion requires an observant attentiveness to other people, it is unavailable to the self-absorbed. And because most of us today are so self-absorbed, we cannot experience compassion toward others. We've even invented a clinical phrase to excuse our self-absorption. Psychologists call it "giving ourselves permission" to focus on ourselves and to "set boundaries." I'm reminded of my friend Marty's little joke about an insufferable person who talks endlessly about himself. After driving his listener to distraction by his total self-absorption he says, "But enough about me—what do *you* think about me?"

5. We Compare Our Suffering

Sometimes we are oblivious to other people's pain because ours is so great. We diminish another person's pain by comparing it to our own. This happened to me when my brother was born with brain damage. His cerebral palsy made other people's problems, including my own, seem unimportant by comparison. I unwittingly became uncaring about any suffering that could not match or exceed Timmy's.

6. We Objectify Suffering

Compassion can give way to apparent apathy when we become overwhelmed by the world's immense suffering. Experts refer to this as "compassion fatigue." Saturated with reports of hunger, famine, or the ravages of war, we shield ourselves from our feelings by quantifying pain statistically or by deciding that these news stories are intended to inform, not move us to action.

7. We Place Blame

Compassion can be displaced by judgmentalism. The Pharisees codified compassionlessness by placing themselves in the role of judge rather than deliverer of mercy to people estranged from God. This same thing can happen today in the guise of a holiness defined as separation from a polluted world or by a culture war defined as an ideological and legislative crusade for proper morality and personal responsibility.

THREE WAYS TO RESTORE YOUR COMPASSION

So how can Christians overcome the obstacles to compassion and regain the spirit of compassion exemplified by Jesus?

1. Recognize God's Compassion for You

Ovid said, "If you want to be loved, become loveable." Thank goodness this is not the basis on which Christ loved us. Christ loved us while we were yet sinners! Having been blessed with the wideness of God's mercy, it is the height of ungratefulness not to exhibit this same mercy toward others. This is why when the scribes complained about Jesus eating with publicans and sinners, Jesus told them to "go and learn what this means, I desire mercy, not sacrifice" (Matthew 9:13). God's love has flowed *to* us so it can flow *through* us.

2. Channel Your Pain

Experience your pain and channel it into compassion for other people. Only those who have experienced suffering can express compassion. As a matter of fact, the word *compassion* finds its etiological roots in the Latin and Greek words for "suffering." These same linguistic elements appear in words like *sympathy* or *empathy*. The compassionate person is one who has experienced pain and has learned through his own pain to recognize and respond when he sees another person in pain. Think of the deepest pain you've experienced in your life: a divorce, the death of someone you love, the birth of a handicapped child, the utter failure to achieve a lifelong dream. These are your personal wellsprings of compassion if you will allow them to be so. And this is the softer side we, Jesus' disciples, can bring to the world.

3. Allow Compassion to Heal You

So long as you nurse, coddle, and dote on your own pain, you cannot move beyond it to serve others. The compassionate person is one who has experienced pain and then translated her own experience into an ability to suffer with others. When you experience suffering and move outside yourself to feel and respond to pain in another person, you release a bit of your own pain.

There is an ancient Hindu parable of a master who grew tired of his apprentice's constant complaining, so he sent him for a glass of water in which he placed a handful of salt and then asked the apprentice to take a drink. The apprentice immediately spit out the bitter water. The master than threw a handful of salt in the lake and asked the apprentice to drink from the lake. When the apprentice observed that this water tasted fresh, the master turned this into a teachable moment. The pain of life is pure salt. The amount of bitterness you taste depends on the container you put the pain in. When you are in pain the only thing you can do is enlarge your sense of things. Stop being the glass. Become the lake.

This is the magic behind Jesus urging us to lose our life to gain it, to lay down our life for our friends. In these counter-intuitive acts we enlarge our "container," and our pain mysteriously becomes less bitter. This expanding cycle of pain absorption extends eternally to God. As the apostle Paul says, "Blessed be the Father of mercies and the God of all consolation, who consoles us in all our affliction, so that we may be able to console those who are in any affliction with the consolation with which we ourselves are consoled by God" (2 Corinthians 1:3–4).

One dictionary defines compassion as "the deep awareness of the suffering of another coupled with a wish to relive it." Touched deeply by God's compassion for us, our deep awareness of the suffering of another can be coupled with a wish to relieve it. The reserves of God's love will enable us to do just that.

CHAPTER 14

■ THINK

I AM AN AGING MAN OF ORDINARY intelligence who loves books, ideas, and concepts. I live in a culture that often devalues these, preferring rather to bestow worth on amusement and commerce. I've spent over a decade in broadcasting, an industry that generally and begrudgingly accepts displays of on-air intelligence only if they are subservient to humor or moderated by outrageous profits. One radio station manager even expressed concern that I was delivering a show too intelligent for Christian radio!

Over thirty years ago Harry Blamires sounded the alarm about the deterioration of the Christian mind in his book *The Christian Mind*, saying, "The mental secularization of Christians means that nowadays we meet only as worshipping beings and as moral beings, not as thinking beings." His warning was updated by Ambassador Charles Malik who said in a 1980 lecture at Wheaton College, "I must be frank with you; the greatest danger besetting American evangelical Christianity is the danger of anti-intellectualism. The mind, as to its greatest and deepest reaches, is not cared for enough."

Then in the 1990s Dr. Mark Noll, in his book *The Scandal of the Evangelical Mind*, issued a clarion call on behalf of a more thoughtful Christian, concluding that the scandal of the evangelical mind is that there is so little of it.

These comments could be set aside as the rants of an elite crew of stuffed shirts were it not for the fact that Jesus commands us to love the Lord our God with all our mind. It is not sufficient to love God with your heart, leaving the "mind" part to smarter people. Loving God with your mind is not just an optional choice, or just for people who listen to classical music and wear tweed with leather elbow patches, or for those with time left over after watching baseball or Oprah. Today's abandonment of the mind is disobedience to God. In *Fit Bodies, Fit Minds*, Os Guinness concludes, "Anti-intellectualism is truly the refusal to love the Lord our God with our minds as required by the first of Jesus' commandments."

I am warning you, in what is generally an anti-intellectual culture and Christian subculture, your commitment to thinking will make you countercultural.

Why is the witness of God's presence in the world of our minds so important?

We Are Created in God's Image

Our minds reflect our status as the only species created in God's image. Our human ability to possess, develop, and express our thoughts in complex language differentiates us from the animals and is evidence of our unique place in God's created order.

WE ARE COMMANDED TO LOVE GOD WITH OUR MINDS

We are commanded to love the Lord our God with body, heart, and mind because each is important to God. This holistic view of human potential was very familiar to the Jewish, Roman, and Greek contemporaries of Jesus. As a matter of fact, the Greek Olympics celebrated *arete*, a word meaning the complete, well-balanced person training to develop body, mind, and spirit. The Greeks would not revere an illiterate athlete or a sedentary academic.

IDEAS HAVE CONSEQUENCES

Karl Marx's political and economic theories ruined millions of lives in the twentieth century. Charles Darwin's evolutionary theory has dominated twentieth century life in overt and subtle ways. As each generation faces the onslaught of novel ideas, Christians in that generation need discerning minds to defend and advance the faith. The apostle Paul says we are not to be conformed to the world's ideas, but to be transformed by the renewing of our minds (Romans 12:2). This discerning mind enables us to weigh the essence and implications of thoughts and ideas gaining contemporary acceptance.

PEOPLE NEED TO HEAR A REASONABLE FAITH

Today we communicate and defend the gospel in an age dominated by scientific naturalism, intellectual and moral relativism, and theological pluralism. A thoughtful approach to each of these is essential if you desire to influence intellectually curious seekers or even to parent your children. Thirty years ago, in his book *The God Who Is There*, Francis Schaeffer observed what happens when this work goes undone. "I find that everywhere I go, children of Christians are being lost to historic Christianity.... They are being lost because their parents are unable to understand their children and therefore cannot help them in their time of need.... We have left the next generation naked in the face of twentieth century thought by which they are surrounded."

SOME PEOPLE WILL COME TO THE FAITH THROUGH THEIR MINDS

We've already mentioned that Aristotle showed the importance of both emotion (*pathos*) and reason (*logos*) in persuasion. While some spiritually restless people will *feel* their way into the kingdom of God, others will *think* their way there. In a 1997 *National Review* article, Frederica Mathewes-Green tells the wonderful story of the Genoveses finding God. Eugene Genovese has enjoyed a brilliant career as a historian, and his wife, Elizabeth, also an academic, helped launch the feminist movement. Together they founded the magazine *Marxist Perspectives*, which was one of many reasons they were dubbed "the royal couple of the radical academic." But their intellectual curiosity and honesty led them down an unexpected path. Eugene tells the story this way.

> In the *Southern Front* I spoke as an atheist; one reviewer said that I protest too much. When the book came off the press and I had to reread it, I started wrestling with the problem philosophically, and I lost.
>
> In the meantime, Betsey was going through her process, and one day announced she'd had a conversion. Now, she and I talk about religion a lot, but for six months we hadn't. So we were doing it separately.
>
> On a philosophical level what I came to decide was that being an atheist involves as great a leap of faith as being a theist. Deep down I think I knew that; it was just my preferred leap of faith. But I was troubled by this even as an undergraduate, when I read the

Brothers Karamazov and encountered Ivan's question; "If there is no God, is not everything permissible?"

There are limits to what we can do to convince and persuade others through sheer intellect. I was reminded of this after Carl Sagan died. Many Christians, leading scientists among them, shared the gospel with Carl Sagan. After his death his widow wanted to reassure everyone that Sagan had no deathbed conversion, that he held firm to his agnosticism to the very end. Kathy Smith's letter to the editor in the next issue of *Newsweek* commented on this:

> I was not surprised to read of Carl Sagan's frustrating intellectual battle over the existence of God. In a culture like ours that deifies intellect and celebrates only that which we can submit to empirical study, there are many who intellectually struggle with the idea of a power greater than ourselves, as if we could prove God is out there and bring him down to our level of human understanding. As marvelous as our brains are, it is my belief that there are bigger and better things than the human intellect. I, for one, am pleased to be amazed by miracles, reduced to tears by unexpected glory, and shaken by the power of God.

A. W. Tozer rightly pointed out that we should not "convince" people into the kingdom, because all it will take to change their mind is someone smarter than us to "convince them back out" of the kingdom. He was not diminishing the importance of mounting a satisfactory apologetic in appealing to people's minds, but was rather identifying the importance of the Holy Spirit dealing with people's wills. Highly intelligent people often reject God, not because they have not heard a reasonable and compelling case for the gospel, but because following Jesus requires them to yield the governance of their life to God.

An Exercise Program for the Mind

To be effective in the world, Jesus' disciples will love God with their minds. Our goal will be the demonstration of our love for God through the engagement of our mind in a rigorous program of mental exercises leading to cultural and biblical literacy.

What might such an exercise program look like?

I suggest you start by identifying, facing, and resolving your own ideological fears. Are there issues being presented in film, music, TV, or water-fountain conversations that trouble you, because you believe they pose a serious threat to your belief system? Identify those issues and seek out answers by reading the Bible and other books and periodicals that address the issue. Expand your intellectual comfort zone by entertaining a broader theological perspective in order to defend or amend your own. Discuss your question with someone who is thoughtful and farther down the spiritual road than you. Pray. Think. And having thoroughly evaluated the issue, reach conclusions that satisfy your mind.

Apply your faith in everyday life. Read newspapers and periodicals and ask yourself how being Christian influences or should influence your thinking on the subject or issue. Read your Bible regularly and slowly and ask how it relates to life and worldviews you faced yesterday or expect to face today. Read beyond your usual fare. Read contemporary fiction as a way of gauging where today's seeker is and what questions they are asking. Ask how the gospel satisfactorily addresses the novelist's concerns.

When you attend films, listen to music, or read a book, ask some basic questions about its theology and worldview. What does it teach or imply about who God is? Who humans are and what our purpose is? What our biggest human problem is? What the solution to our problem is? What the future will hold for humans? Then ask how the worldview you've identified compares and contrasts with a Christian worldview.

If you disagree with what your pastor or teacher says at church or at a Bible study, review your own stance, make sure you can defend it, then graciously confront them and ask them to defend their position! On occasion I've asked listeners to call anonymously and tell me what they know they're supposed to believe but don't believe. Every time I've done this I've been deluged with calls from Christians who passively listen to sermons or teaching they disagree with, but never raise their objections or wrestle the issue through to a reasonable conclusion

Join a book club or one of the discussion groups popping up at local bookstores. Listen, think, express your views. Get comfortable with the give and take. Go back to school or talk with your kids about what they're studying in school. Volunteer to teach a class of teenagers and get them to raise their real questions. It will drive you to thinking and praying. Take an extension course from a Christian university or seminary and expand your understanding of your own faith.

Be a lifelong learner. Love God with your mind. And prepare to give a reason for the hope that lives within you (1 Peter 3:15).

TAILOR YOUR MESSAGE

THE RIGHT WORDS, SPOKEN CLEARLY, will pierce the hearer's soul with laserlike precision. Communicating the gospel more effectively does not require more words, but better listening, and then selecting the most suitable words. We will not accept a surgeon whose scalpel is only in the vicinity of its mark, nor should we accept the sloppy wielding of life-giving words.

Jesus never presented the gospel the same way twice. His application of the gospel was always tailored to the individual to whom he spoke. This is why he could so quickly bring each person to a moment of decision. Tailoring the gospel requires you to understand the way another person lives and thinks and the questions raised by their life problems. This means you must participate in their lives.

Because the gospel is multidimensional and people's situations are unique, if you want to be effective you will need to calibrate the presentation of the gospel to an individual's needs. Think of a NASA spacecraft docking with the space station thousands of miles out there in space. Docking the two crafts requires a fine-tuned, precise meshing of the two ships. This same fit is what happens when we have tailored the gospel to match an individual's point of receptivity. This tailoring will not always result in their decision to embrace the gospel, but it increases the likelihood that they will make a definite decision for or against it.

TAILOR YOUR MESSAGE

As a new missionary in Africa, Charles Kraft learned that if you win the chief, you've won the village, so he was excited to gain a hearing with the chief. In this first meeting Kraft asked, "Chief, what would you say if I told you the Jesus I serve was risen from the dead?"

"That's no big deal—my cousin Bruno has been raised from the dead," the chief replied.

Kraft was taken aback by the chief's reply. Inquiring further, Kraft discovered that if someone recovered after being knocked unconscious, they were considered a survivor of death. Obviously, Kraft could no longer use the Resurrection as the point of entry for presenting the gospel to the village. This was a serious moment for Kraft. He was offering a solution for a problem the chief did not think he had!

Fortunately, Kraft did a most sensible thing. He asked a follow-up question. "Chief, if being raised from the dead isn't good news, what would be good news?"

The chief replied, "If there was someone who had power over the evil spirits, this would be good news indeed."

Kraft said, "Chief, what if I told you this Jesus who has been raised from the dead has power over all the spirit world?"

The chief replied, "That would be good news indeed."

This story illustrates the importance of tailoring our presentation of truth to our hearer. This is not to say we change or eliminate key beliefs of our faith. Certainly Kraft holds to the centrality and historicity of the Resurrection. But Kraft learned he was more effective after discovering the chief's needs. He then could show the relevance of the gospel for that need. The chief was unimpressed with the concept of the Resurrection until it was linked to what he was truly concerned about—the spirit world. Through identifying that concern, Kraft found the most effective way to show Jesus' relevance to the chief's life. This tailoring of the gospel caused a "fit."

Stores like Nordstrom develop a profile of each customer so they know just what kind of item will be of interest to the customer. As anyone who shops Amazon.com knows, once you've made a purchase, you will start receiving information about other books on the same subject. At Blockbuster Video, you rent a movie and there is often a shelf below saying, "If you liked that movie, maybe you should try this one."

By listening to your seeking friends, you can develop an informal profile of who they are and what they are concerned about. Those personal concerns are the doorways you can enter with conversations about Jesus' relevance for your friend's life. Let me illustrate this by telling you the story of my friend Julian.

A GIFT FOR JULIAN

It was the summer of 1979, and yours truly was entering a high-rise penthouse with a dramatic, sweeping view of San Francisco Bay. I was there for the birthday of my friend Julian, a gay coworker. Also invited were sixty gay men and four straight women. Greeting me warmly, Julian exuberantly kissed me on both cheeks. Taking a deep breath, I ventured into a scene that gave a whole new meaning to the phrase "sea of humanity." By now I don't even need to tell you that for some of my too-Christian friends, just attending this party made me way too pagan.

I wore white slacks that night, a detail I recall only because I discovered belatedly this was the seasonal color of choice in the Castro district's fashion-conscious gay boutiques. A man on a mission, I was an accidental, unintentional hit. And as I had so many times before when crossing cultures, I chuckled quietly, asking myself a familiar question: "What in the world am I doing here?"

Actually I knew exactly why I was there, having prayed with some friends for a desirable outcome just a few hours earlier. I've always thought of events like Julian's party as "wedding feast of Cana" situations. You'll recall Jesus performed his first miracle at that first-century party packed with pagans. He turned the regular old water into a fine wine, making a dramatic kingdom impact on the party-goers. Even more significant, though, was how Jesus turned an ordinary event into an extraordinary opportunity to focus attention on God's kingdom.

Before the party I tried to think through how to be there for Jesus. In the case of Julian's party, the selection of the right gift was the place to start. I saw it as an opportunity to tailor the gospel and provoke a discussion leading to a response. What do you buy for a gay, Jewish, agnostic millionaire who has everything except the one thing he really wants and needs—a personal relationship with the living God?

I knew Julian was conflicted about his Jewishness. His gay life had brought him a great deal of personal suffering, physically, relationally, and emotionally. I also knew he loved art and loved to read.

So my assignment was to find a book that wove together themes of Jewishness, suffering, art, and also inserted Jesus into the mix! Amazingly, such a book had just been published. After I read *The Chosen* and *The Promise,* Chaim Potok became one of my favorite authors. Most of his books feature a central character struggling with the restrictions of life in the Jewish fundamentalism of the Hasidim. Reading these books had provided a new lens through which to view my own experience with Christian legalism.

At the time of Julian's party, Potok had just released *My Name Is Asher Lev.* It tells the story of a young Hasidic boy who, though a gifted artist, is not allowed to draw because of restrictions on making graven images. Finally, forced to choose between his artistic gift, his family, and his faith tradition, the young man leaves home and eventually becomes a successful artist. The book climaxes with the father visiting a New York gallery to view his son's crowning achievement, a painting about a suffering son. The father is shocked to see the subject matter his son has chosen to communicate the greatest suffering known to man—it was a painting of the crucifixion of Jesus.

I gave the book to Julian as I left the party late Friday night. Monday Julian asked if we could talk. He had read the book over the weekend and was deeply moved by the way it connected to his own life as a Jewish, gay man acquainted with suffering. I'd love to tell you that Julian decided to follow Jesus. He did not. But the selection of the book was tailored in such a way that it connected at every point of Julian's sojourn and therefore opened doors for me to show the relevance of the gospel for his life.

LEARN TO LISTEN

Knowing how to tailor the gospel's presentation requires careful observation and that most basic of communication skills, listening. In a *Prism* magazine editorial, Dwight Ozard said we've lost our ability to listen. "We want to reach people without listening, without the hard work of straining to hear what lies beyond the interminable racket and crass immediacy that is their language, without being touched by their fears and without understanding the roots of their rebellions and cynicisms. We are more likely to be scandalized than broken-hearted by their rootlessness and self-destruction, blinded by their promiscuities to the hungerings beyond them. All the while we wonder why they won't listen. Punch line: Or as Jesus might have said, Let those who have ears to hear, shut up and listen."

As you think about your friends, or as you cross cultures to make new friends, let me assure you of this. Your sharing of the gospel will be enhanced when you participate in an individual life, listen carefully, and then tailor your presentation of the gospel to that person's needs.

CHAPTER 16

LEARN THE ART OF DUAL LISTENING

EFFECTIVELY TAILORING OUR MESSAGE requires the disciple of Jesus to be an active dual listener. If you are not listening or cannot understand what the seeker is articulating, how can you tailor the message so he or she can hear it? Anyone who has traveled abroad knows how frustrating it is to not speak or understand the local language. A disciple of Jesus should feel the same frustration if he or she speaks only one language. Because we are citizens of two kingdoms, a disciple will be driven to understand and speak both the language of faith and the language of culture.

John Stott refers to this practice as "dual listening." In his book *Contemporary Christian*, he defines dual listening as hearing both God's Word and the world's need. Stott says, "Bad listeners do not make good disciples." Dual listening enables you to understand, live out, and defend your faith in a world of ideas and values that are alien and sometimes hostile to your faith. While pastoring All Souls Church in London, Stott helped people cultivate these skills by convening a film-watchers group. The group would view a film, reconvene at a pub, and engage in some wrestling with the film's message in the context of the gospel. Way ahead of his time, Stott hosted book groups of laypeople who met to discuss the ideas conveyed in best-selling books, always with an eye toward how to live out and communicate faith in the context of those ideological influences.

LEARN TO EXEGETE

Our son Joshua grew so weary of my desire to help him understand the meaning of films that at the age of ten he once wailed, "Why do we always have to talk about the meaning of the film? Can't we just enjoy it?" The answer was "No!"

Today many people would like to just enjoy the entertainment value of culture without engaging in any analysis, but it is dangerous and irresponsible to do so. The apostle Paul admonishes us to "take every thought captive to obey Christ" (2 Corinthians 10:5), which requires us to be attentive to the philosophies conveyed. This has never been more important because there are powerful, underlying worldviews and ideas conveyed in popular entertainment. Without careful, attentive dual listening, worldviews hostile to the gospel may enter our minds and lives like ideological enemies concealed in a Trojan horse.

Dual listening requires learning the skills of exegesis. To *exegete* means to "perceive quickly, explain, critically analyze or interpret a word or literary passage." When engaged in dual listening, you will want to analyze and assess both the cultural message and the gospel message and then compare and contrast the two.

BE BILINGUAL

In addition to listening interpretively you will also want to be "bilingual." By this, I mean you need to be able to speak the gospel in the seeker's language. It would not occur to a missionary in a foreign setting to attempt to share the gospel without gaining a rudimentary foundation in the local language and culture. Neither should we attempt to influence people in our country without understanding their subculture, vocabulary, and customs. Madison Avenue spends millions of dollars to identify just the right phrase or visual image to connect with their target audience. We face the even more daunting challenge of translating first-century gospel language for the contemporary ear.

INCREASE YOUR BIBLICAL LITERACY

Dual listening and bilingual communication both require a biblical literacy. Unfortunately, all the research shows that we are a society buying Bibles but seldom reading them.

In a 1997 *Christianity Today* article, John Stackhouse recounts a story illustrating biblical illiteracy even among the well-educated.

> "Who is this 'apostle Paul' you're referring to?"
> I was sitting quietly, thunderstruck at 35,000 feet. On a flight from Chicago to Minneapolis, I had been talking to my seatmate. A young executive on her way to a new job, she had told me a little about herself. Among other things, I found that she had earned university degrees from Ivy League Dartmouth College and from the internationally recognized business school at the University of Chicago.

She, in turn, had asked me about my work and I had joked that some of my introductory students could not place Jesus and the apostle Paul in the correct chronological order. "Who is this 'apostle Paul' you're referring to?" she asked me, utterly sincere, completely unaware that this ought to be an embarrassing question for a well-schooled American to ask.

It is amusing to hear children convoluting basic Bible stories, but what are we to make of church-going adults, who, when quizzed, believe Noah was married to Joan of Arc or can't name the four gospels? George Barna reports that 80 percent of adults he surveyed said the most famous quote in the Bible was "God helps those who help themselves." This is actually a quote from Thomas Jefferson.

WHERE DO I START?

Dual listening, exegesis, bilingualism, biblical literacy—you may be saying, "This sounds like a lot of work! To do what you're saying would require me to learn a lot more about culture or the Bible, or both!"

I do think this is a challenging task, but we must do this work or our faith risks being swept under the tide of alien ideas rushing into our lives each day. Engage in dual listening and bilingualism, or give up any possibility of articulating a vibrant, relevant faith to your circle of influence.

Because your heart is moved with the kind of compassion Jesus displayed for seekers, because you have truly experienced fellowship with the living God, and because you have committed to follow Jesus, I am confident you will want to do whatever it takes to communicate the gospel to people around you.

So where do you start? Maybe you should start where John Stott did. Get a group together to read best-sellers and then discuss them, or go to the movies together and talk about where the films intersect with issues of faith. Start a small group to discuss issues about faith raised by popular magazines. Read the article, search Scripture for some insight into the issue, and then prepare to share your findings and questions with the group. These and other activities like them will help you and your fellow Christians learn the art of dual listening and will equip you to discuss these issues intelligently with your friends.

Dual listening is especially important for the next generation, which, as Tom Beaudoin says in *Virtual Faith*, was "born in the amniotic fluid of popular culture." As I pointed out earlier, "Generation Next" is largely disconnected from organized religion. Given their decreased interest in organized religion and increased interest in spiritual questions, where are they answering their theological questions? In the popular culture. If you want to communicate the gospel to young people, an awareness of their music, films, and books is a necessity, not an option.

LISTEN TO THE MUSIC

W WHILE IN COLLEGE I WAS ON STAFF AT Peninsula Covenant Church, and during seminary I served on the staff of Park Street Church in Boston. In both these settings you'd find me "exegeting" music with high school students. I find many students begin to see the relevance of the Bible when they analyze its teachings in the context of the ideas they confront every day in pop culture. So, we'd listen to "Jesus Christ Superstar," "Bridge Over Troubled Water," "Jesus Is Just Alright," or "Spirit in the Sky," and then break into small groups to look for the theology in the lyrics.

I want you to do the same work I've encouraged these students to do, especially if you have kids or are in daily contact with people immersed in the pop music culture. A lot of garbage is produced by the record labels, but there is also some wonderful stuff. Listening to music requires a commitment to dual listening. You'll need to compare the music and lyrics to the values of your faith vigorously and vigilantly. You simply cannot allow lyrics to enter your brain without filtering them through the process of dual listening.

WHAT NEED IS BEING MET BY THE MUSIC?

Our neighbor's twenty-year-old son recently committed suicide. The day before he died Nathaniel cranked up the volume on some of the vilest, most self-loathing, hostile sounds I've ever heard. Though not knowing the young man because we had just moved into the neighborhood, I commented to my son that anyone listening to that music must really be hurting. The next day the boy took his life. A few weeks later the boy's father and I were talking and I asked him about the music. His dad said, "I hated the music, but it clearly communicated what my son felt—a deep, deep pain."

By listening carefully to popular music, you'll begin to understand the themes of different segments or subcultures of our society, and you'll begin to understand the mental and spiritual condition of the artists and the kids who resonate with their art. Whenever you don't understand the popularity of a given artist, you need simply ask "What need in the listener is being met by this artist?"

The reason so many kids (and adults for that matter) listen to so much truly awful stuff is that it fits what they feel inside and connects with them at a very deep level. In 1999, *Newsweek*, in a feature about today's teens, concluded, "Kids are immersed in a universe outside their parents' reach, a world defined by computer games, TV, and movies. Ninety-six percent of high school kids listen to CDs or tapes an average of 9.9 hours a week." Music is a place kids go to work out their beliefs and feelings.

I'd like to suggest we use music as a window to the questions people are asking and to the contemporary theological responses to those questions.

The lyrics exegete will find a range of messages in today's music. Books like Walt Mueller's *Understanding Today's Youth Culture*, Bob De Moss's *Learn to Discern*, Focus on the Family's *Chart Watch*, or Steve Peter's *Truth About Rock* all devote considerable attention to the evil and dangers lurking in so much of today's music. Sex, suicide and depression, drugs and alcohol, hatred of parents or anyone else in authority—all these are regular themes in today's popular music and a diet of this stuff can be hazardous to your health. Youth culture experts observe common themes of loneliness, and a desire for personal meaning and significance.

Perhaps of greatest interest for our purposes is a brief overview of some of the theology emerging from contemporary music. By understanding the issues, themes, and theology of the music, we'll be better equipped to tailor the gospel to fit the specific issues of the listener to that music.

Identifying theology in today's music is pretty easy, because the music scene is dominated by lyrics revealing the spiritual search of this generation.

PROPHETIC VOICES

There are prophetic voices on the music scene. In 1995 Don Henley's record company asked him for a "sparkly ballad." He told them, "Well, I'm sorry, I'm not in a sparkly mood" and instead offered them "The Garden of Allah," an incredibly scathing analysis of society during the height of the O.J. trial. It tells a tale in which the devil visits a large Western city (LA) and finds that he has become obsolete. The song touches on the folly of moral relativism and the general deterioration of American society in a way that could have emerged straight from the Bible.

Calling LA "Gomorrah-by-the-sea," the devil comments, "It's just like home." He bemoans the fact that there was a time when good was good and evil was evil, before things got so "fuzzy." In references to the O.J. debacle, the devil says, "It was a dark, dark night on the collective soul when the people gave their blessing to crimes of passion." Then the devil talks about an expert witness in the trial who promises he can get any result desired, because "there are no facts, there is no truth, just data to be manipulated, there is no wrong, there is no right." The witness says he sleeps well at night, "no shame, no remorse, no retribution, just people selling T-shirts, just the opportunity to participate in the pathetic little circus and winning, winning, winning." The song ends with the downhearted devil slithering off the scene, concluding his work is done, "there's nothing left to claim."

Metallica's *And Justice for All* shows a similar wistfulness at the loss of values in society.

> When a man lies, he murders some part of the world
> These are the pale deaths which men call their lives
> All this I cannot bear to witness any longer
> Cannot the kingdom of salvation take me home.

Both Don Henley and Metallica are giving voice to the deep feelings that things aren't the way they're supposed to be. Such anguished admissions provide remarkable openings for conversation about the way things are, why they are that way, the way they're supposed to be, and what the gospel says can be done about it.

AGNOSTIC VOICES

There is agnosticism reflected in artists like the aging James Taylor, who dubbed his *Hourglass* "spirituals for agnostics."

The lyrics for "Up from Your Life" reflect a spiritual search that rejects Christian teaching.

> So much for your moment of prayer
> God's not at home, There is no one there.
> Lost in the stars, That's what you are
> Left here on your own.
> You can only hope to live on this earth
> This here is it, for all it's worth
> Nothing else awaits you
> No second birth, No starry crown.
> For an unbeliever like you
> There's not much they can do.

Taylor instead embraces neopaganism, as shown in the lyrics for the song "Gaia."

> Pray for the forest pray to the tree
> Pray for the fish in the deep blue sea
> Pray for yourself and for God's sake
> Say one for me
> Poor, wretched unbeliever.
> Someone's got to stop us now
> Save us from us, Gaia.

SACRED AND PROFANE

Today's music often reflects a confusing combination of the sacred with the profane and sensual. Salt N' Pepa's Cheryl James talks openly about being sexual without losing the focus of her Christian faith saying in a 1997 *Newsweek* article, "I can look sexy, have a good time, and still be praising God."

In Joan Osborne's best-selling song "One of Us," she asks, "What if God was one of us, just a slob like one of us? Just a stranger on the bus? Trying to make his way home." She then followed with a single "Right Hand Man," which she says fulfills part of her mission to "reconcile the ancient mind-body split." In this song about a woman looking for spiritual and sexual liberation "she bops down the street the morning after a sexual conquest, panties in a wad at the bottom of her purse, finding the reconciliation right where she needs it, in her own neighborhood."

Madonna's "Like a Prayer" is also a mix of sacred and sensual. And Courtney Love's 1999 concert at Hollywood's Viper Room included a show opened by Hindu yoga chants. Then Love came on stage, kicked one leg up on an amp, clutched prayer beads in one hand and a cigarette in the other, and launched into Guns n' Roses "Paradise City."

HOSTILE VOICES

Then there are artists openly hostile to Christianity. Tori Amos says she is on a mission to expose the dark side of Christianity and regularly provokes Christians with her outrageous proclamations, as shown in her interview with Joe Jackson in *Hot Press.*

> I've always believed that Jesus really liked Mary Magdalene and that if he was as he claimed to be, a whole man, he had to have sexual relations with her. So in my private moments I've wanted Christ to be the boyfriend I've been waiting for. I may have felt guilty at the thought of wanting to do it with Jesus, but then I say, why not? He *was* a man.

Marilyn Manson, who has described himself as "Satan's little helper," released the dark *Antichrist Superstar.* In a 1996 *Metal Edge* article, he declared, "Each age has to have at least one brave individual that tried to bring an end to Christianity, which no one has managed to succeed yet, but maybe through music we can finally do it."

SPIRITUAL LONGING

There are also songs about genuine spiritual longing and searching, like Sheryl Crow's "Maybe Angels," which offers a tabloid-like overview of contemporary questing. She talks about taking the six-lane highway down to Pensacola where she meets a bunch of holy rollers who "don't know nothin' about saving me." She then journeys to Roswell, New Mexico, where she packs her bags to wait for aliens who she believes may come to take her away. Finally, she talks about her sister's communication with the dead, wailing "my sister she says she knows Elvis, she knows Jesus, John Lennon and Cobain personally." Not sure of the identity of the transcendent she nevertheless returns to the refrain, "I swear they're out there, swear they're out there, maybe angels."

CHRISTIANITY MISUNDERSTOOD

Throughout today's popular music we see bad theology sure to disappoint the seeker often combined with misunderstandings about Christianity. In a 1998 *Rolling Stone* article, Paula Cole talks about a "spiritual breakthrough" that led her to understand that "God doesn't exist." She says, "I don't want to get into it. It's too private. But I know it with every cell. If you look at a blade of grass, you can see that all things are interrelated . . . And my life had meaning."

People magazine says of Jewel's foray into the spiritual, "Tis the season, apparently, for pop lessons in New Age metaphysics. On the heels of releases from the newly spiritual Madonna and Alanis Morissette, Jewel Kilcher follows. She sings her creed in songs like 'Innocence Maintained': 'We will all be Christed when we hear ourselves say, We are that to which we pray.'"

Sarah McLachlan longs for true communion in songs like "I Will Remember You," but she also reflects a confused theology. In an interview published in *Details* magazine in 1998, she says, "I think the devil has gotten a bad rap. The devil is the fallen angel, the one who was willing to embrace his dark side, whereas all the other angels were in total denial. The devil is more like us—we're all the devil and we're all God."

Sadly, many of these artists were exposed to Christianity at a young age. Tori Amos's grandmother and father were ministers, Sheryl Crow was active in Young Life, Marilyn Manson was raised in a fundamentalist home and even attended private Christian schools for a few years, and Joan Osborne is a lapsed Catholic who left the church at age eight or nine.

Unfortunately, these artists often misunderstand or mischaracterize Christian teaching. Tori Amos says in a 1998 *Rolling Stone* article, "The problem with Christianity is they think everything is outside forces—good and evil. With Christianity there's not a lot of inner work encouraged." Sinead O'Connor, recently ordained in the Tridentine Order of the Catholic Church, went through a Rastafarian phase rejecting Christianity because, as she said in a 1997 *Time* article, "The people of the Christian church teach that God is dead and we can never be like God."

In a rant in a 1999 *Rolling Stone* magazine, Marilyn Manson tried to blame the violence at Columbine on Christianity because, "Whether you interpret the Bible as literature or as the final word of whatever God may be, Christianity has given us an image of death and sexuality that we have based our culture around. A half-naked dead man hangs in most homes and around our necks, and we have just taken that for granted all our lives. . . . The world's most famous murder suicide was also the birth of the death icon—the blueprint for celebrity. Unfortunately, for all of their inspiring morality, nowhere in the gospels is intelligence praised as a virtue."

In a 1996 *Rolling Stone* article, Joan Osborne talks about her spiritual search in India and her belief that "organized religion doesn't allow you to come to God or spirituality with all of yourself, with your brain and your will and your curiosity and your sensuality and everything."

In each case these comments reflect a misunderstanding of Christianity, willful or otherwise, that colors the artist's opinions and is perpetuated when their adoring followers, often lacking in discernment, accept their hero's attacks as reasons they too should reject and even despise Christianity.

Given this rather grim overview of the theological frenzy in today's music, what is the follower of Jesus to do in such a world?

UNDERSTAND THE QUESTIONS

First, we need to understand the questions raised in today's music and be prepared to show how the gospel applies today. The group LIVE states this emphatically in their song, "Operation Spirit."

Heard a lot about this Jesus
    A man of love, a man of strength
But what a man was two thousand years ago
Means nothing at all to me today.
He could have been telling me about my higher self
But he only lives inside my prayer
    So what he said may have been beautiful
But the pain is right now and right here.

The gospel with its offer of a personal experience with the living God, mediated by Jesus who understands our sorrows, lives today and offers love in a new community of friends—this should be good news to a lonely generation, weary of suffering.

PREPARE AN ANSWER

Second, we need to know the futile spiritual paths and misunderstandings about Christianity and be prepared to steer people toward the truth.

Many of these distorted views of our faith probably grow out of the teaching the artist received and rejected earlier in life. The artist may bear deep emotional and psychological scars that were inflicted in the name of God and Christianity.

One of our biggest challenges is to liberate people from their distorted *religious* experience of Christianity so we can introduce them to the *spiritual* vibrancy of the gospel.

Tori's fans need to know Christianity does encourage "inner work." Sinead's can be reassured that we believe "God is alive." Marilyn Manson's devotees should know that our faith encourages intelligence, as evidenced by Jesus' call to love God and each other with our "minds." Osborne should be pleased to know that God is the creator of all things and celebrates everything about her, "brain, will, sensuality and everything."

Knowing the lyrics and theology of contemporary music and then framing responses is particularly important as we deal with our kids who are inevitably exposed, either directly or through their peers, to the ideas and values carried in popular music. A restrictive *legalism* will cause our kids to rebel. *Permissiveness* is irresponsible, naïve, and will make our kids vulnerable to the sinister forces at work in the lyrics. Our path is that of *discernment*, produced by a dual listening and a genuine love for our kids and the lost artists they so often admire.

Listen to the music.

CHAPTER 18

SEE THE MOVIE

SECLUDED IN DARKNESS AND SILENCE (except for the too-loud, nearby crunching of popcorn), we are completely immersed for two hours in another world. We are absorbed in someone else's story, in their place and perspective. For the moment we cannot shape, but are enveloped in a one-directional communication. Their world becomes our world. But as the lights come up, we, Jesus' disciples, should have already set about the task of comparing the filmmaker's worldview to our own. In our subsequent reflections and conversations we respect the integrity of the film-maker's vision but interpret it within the context of our own, making parabolic use of it in our understanding and communication of the gospel.

When I think about Jesus being moved with compassion, I often think of incidents in movie theatres where I felt, within my own spirit, his agony for bruised and hurting people.

I think of the time I saw the international, award-winning film *Antonia's Line*, a film that deals explicitly with lesbianism. The theatre was on Seattle's Capital Hill, a place popular with gays. Sitting in the packed theatre, watching what I thought was a very sad film, I could not stop thinking about God's love for these people and the cultural barriers that would keep them from entering most churches. I thought about the almost daily attacks on gays in Christian broadcasting, and I asked myself, "Who will reach these people and how?"

I viewed *Good Will Hunting* in a Harvard Square theatre packed with twenty-somethings (and me, a fifty-year-old!). The film juxtaposes Matt Damon's character—an uncultured guy who happens to be a mathematical savant—and his profanity-laced, blue-collar Boston buddies with the intellectually elitist MIT and Harvard crowd. His romance with a Harvard woman, played by Minnie Driver, is a central dynamic in the movie, showing Damon struggling with the sometimes incompatible twin destinies of love and profession. At a pivotal moment in the film, Driver wants a confirmation of his love and Damon refuses to give it. The row of women behind me started to sob. They weren't alone. Throughout the theatre you could hear the sadness of a generation.

I thought of what Dieter Zander said, earlier that same day. He told me of this generation's feelings of alienation and pain and of their simultaneous yearning for and fear of love. I thought of a "Christian" review of this film I had read, discouraging Christians from seeing it because of its profanity. And I asked myself, "Who will reach these people and how?"

My friend Cliff Taulbert wrote the wonderful book *Once Upon a Time When We Were Colored*. When it was released as a film I wanted to see it. Sadly, this literary gem didn't receive wide distribution and in Chicago was showing only in a predominately black neighborhood. I asked a film-loving, politically liberal, suburbanite, white guy to go to the film with me and he agreed. I forgot to tell him where the film was showing. The minute I took the freeway exit his reaction was immediate. "What are you doing? Have you lost your mind? Do you know where we are? Let's get out of here."

I sedated him with calming verbiage, bought our tickets, and entered a theatre nicely filled with an all-black audience. We were the only whites there. Our minority status made the film all the more poignant. The depiction of a minority black subculture trying to maintain dignity in a white-owned Southern plantation touched me deeply. When the film was over, I felt empathy with the audience, but the silence as we left the theatre symbolized the strained relations between the races. I asked myself, "How can Jesus heal and bridge this great divide?"

THE POWER OF MOVIES

Film has tremendous influence on our culture. *Entertainment Weekly* said in 1999, "Today's media is the most powerful mythology-creating medium ever invented." In a 1996 *TV Guide* interview, Susan Sarandon said of film, "Film and TV shows have so much influence; they can define the expectation of what it means to be a man or woman, of what's fun and what's not, of what is acceptable and what's not."

Both in the U.S. and abroad, American films wield such enormous influence that in 1997 the China scholar Orville Schell observed in the *New York Times*, "Hollywood is the most powerful force in the world, besides the U.S. military." A 1999

Newsweek poll showed that 98 percent of teens watch TV or films every week, an average of eleven hours a week. This generation views the world through the lens of pop culture. Their conversation is peppered with frequent references to film, music, an episode of *Seinfeld* or *Friends*, or a slogan from an ad campaign.

While such power can be used for good, overall most would agree that Hollywood has tilted toward its darker angels in the selection of subject matter and themes. Woody Allen once quipped, "In Hollywood they don't take out the garbage, they make it into a TV series." Filmmaker John Waters, when asked in an NPR interview about the culture war, said, "There is no culture war. Hollywood won, and we're exporting American trash culture to the world!" After the tragic shootings at Columbine, CBS boss Les Moonves commented, "Anybody who doesn't pay attention to what is going on and says the media has nothing to do with this is an idiot." There is no question that Hollywood regularly promotes values straight from the dark side, and indiscriminate consumption of its products can be detrimental to one's health.

That is why so often the most highly visible Christian responses to Hollywood are from activists, naysayers, and handwringers who take on Hollywood as an ideological enemy. Donald Wildmon's American Family Association organizes boycotts against Disney and others, the Catholic League protests *Dogma* and other anti-Catholic productions, and Jerry Falwell rails about everything from the violence of *The Matrix* (missing all its rich theological themes) to the gayness of Tinky Winky.

While in many cases these reactions are understandable, it concerns me that many Christians think, and Hollywood perceives, that we are only adversarial in our relationship with them. This concerns me for two reasons. First, as a dual listening, discerning viewer, I love film. As an art form it is designed to elicit a response, and with me it often succeeds.

Hollywood produces trash, anti-religious, and mindless escapist films, but Hollywood also produces gems, capable of transporting us beyond our own world, introducing us to warm, wild, colorful, disturbing characters and to exotic, dazzling places and to paradigm-shifting themes. Film's ability to offer a vicarious interaction with these broader worlds can help us understand other people, different cultures, and ourselves, and in so doing can enrich and add texture to our life and faith.

Second, rather than bemoaning Hollywood's inevitable and irreversible influence, I would like us to harness it for the kingdom. Hollywood has a tradition of forming strategic alliances with Christians to suit its purposes. The producers of *Chariots of Fire* arranged prescreenings for pastors and other Christian leaders to get advance word of mouth support for the film, which translated into a strong box office and an Academy award. Dreamworks, producers of *Prince of Egypt,* asked Ted Baehr, president of the Christian Film and Television Commission, to arrange for input from Old and New Testament scholars in the writing of the script. Then they arranged advance screenings for Christian leaders.

Isn't turnabout fair play? Shouldn't Jesus' followers discover ways to harness Hollywood for God's kingdom? Let me suggest some ways we can do just that.

USE FILM TO UNDERSTAND CULTURE

First, we can harness film right now by engaging it as a language through which to understand culture and communicate the gospel. Allow me to explain. In the first century the gospel spread for a variety of reasons, but from a tactical standpoint, high on the list was the Roman contribution of a common language and road system, which expedited both gospel messengers and the message. The Roman road system allowed the apostles to travel the world quickly, and the common language meant the apostles could communicate wherever their travels took them.

Today, technologies like the Web, satellites, computers, and TVs are the road system on which messages travel expeditiously. And pop culture is one of only three common languages spoken in today's world. (The other two are money and English.)

Let me illustrate how pop culture has become a common language. In 1998 while in remote Kunming, China, I was interviewed by a twenty-year-old Chinese woman who hosted a show entirely devoted to American pop culture. In the Middle East, I've seen Bedouin tents equipped with satellite dishes for TV and VCRs for video. Hikmut Ongan, an entrepreneur, opened a bagel shop in Turkey, a country where people had never eaten bagels. It was an immediate success. Why? People in Turkey saw Bruce Willis eat bagels in *Die Hard II,* and Hikmut knew there would be a sudden demand for them. Michael Jordan, Sylvester Stallone, Sharon Stone, Clint Eastwood—all are household names around the world.

Film gives us a picture of the questions people are asking and the contemporary theological responses to those questions. Our ability to communicate the gospel is enhanced when we know how to frame it to fit our audience. Film helps us do that because pop culture is where people are raising life issues and working out their theology.

I already mentioned how *Antonia's Line, Good Will Hunting,* and *Once Upon a Time When We Were Colored* touched on contemporary issues for me. There are countless thoughtful and often exceedingly popular films that offer insight into contemporary issues. In a period of one year, filmmakers released *Deep Impact, Armageddon,* and *Contact.* Why? All these films tap into millennial themes, and people are curious and sometimes anxious about what's going to happen in the new millennium. *The Thirteenth Floor, The Matrix,* and other films asked what is real and how can we know it is real. *City of Angels, The Sixth Sense, Ghost, Always, Meet Joe Black,* and *What Dreams May Come* all treated the subject of life after death. *Stigmata, The Exorcist,* and *The Devil's Advocate* probed beliefs about the supernatural and spirit world. *Things That Matter Most* dealt with mother/daughter relationships and changing perceptions of the role of women.

Film is also a picture of today's theology. It helps us understand what people believe about God and man's relationship with God. In a 1999 *Time* interview with George Lucas, Bill Moyers concluded, "The Bible no longer occupies the central place in our culture. Young people in particular are turning to movies for their inspiration, not to organized religion." George Lucas, however, discourages the substitution of pop culture for organized religion. "I hope that doesn't end up being the course the whole thing takes, because I think there's definitely a place for organized religion. I would hate to find ourselves in a completely secular world where entertainment was passing for some kind of religious experience."

Cultural observer Alexander Theroux summarize the Star Wars situation this way in a 1999 *Wall Street Journal* editorial: "Make no mistake, this is a religion, with Lucas as God, the multiplex as church, and rabid fans as fevered acolytes who can both 'witness' the 'truth' and later show their good faith by bringing their custom to outlying stores, their essential parish."

We may not like the trend away from organized religion and toward pop culture theology, but it is a reality, especially for the younger generation. By becoming conversant with film, we can understand the issues our peers are wrestling with, and parents can get insight into their own kids.

Star Wars is just one obvious example of a film constructed with intricate and intentional mythologies, including a distinct messianic character. In *The Phantom Menace* we learn that Darth Vader (Anakin) was born of a virgin, not of a father, but of the Midi-chlorians, the link between every living thing and the Force. The priestly Jedi are aware of an ancient prophecy that a "chosen one will appear and alter the Force forever, bringing balance between darkness and light."

Alex Wainer of Milligan College said in a 1999 *Chicago Sun Times* article, "Lucas has taken all the religions, put them in a blender, and hit the button."

This is no surprise when you know what Lucas has said about his own theological sojourn. In the Moyers interview, Lucas said, "I remember when I was ten years old, I asked my mother, 'If there's only one God, why are there so many religions?' I've been wondering that ever since, and the conclusion I've reached is that all religions are true."

When asked if one religion is as good as another Lucas said, "I would say so.... I think there is a God. No question. What that God is or what we know about that God, I'm not sure. The one thing I know about life and about the human race is that we've always tried to construct some kind of context for the unknown. Even the cavemen thought they had it figured out. I would say that cavemen understood on a scale of about 1. Now we've made it up to 5. The only thing most people don't realize is the scale goes to 1 million."

The Matrix is rich with religious themes, from Neo, the chosen one, to a messianic spaceship called Nebuchadnezzar on a search for the lost city of Zion. In *Simon Birch* we meet the congenitally dwarf-sized Simon, who believes that God has a specific plan and destiny for his life. His best friend, Joe, comes to believe in God through his friendship with Simon.

On the television front, Matt Groening, creator of *The Simpsons,* said in an *Orlando Sentinel* interview, "Right wingers complain there's no God on TV. Not only do the Simpsons go to church every Sunday and pray, they actually speak to God from time to time." Executive producer Mike Scully says, "*The Simpsons* is consistently irreverent toward organized religion's failings and excesses. However, God is not mocked. When the characters are faced with crises, they turn to God. He answers their prayers and intervenes in their world." *Prism,* the magazine of Evangelicals for Social Action agrees, publishing comments by Bill Dark, a teacher who says the series is the "most pro-family, God-preoccupied, home-based program on TV. There is more prayer on *The Simpsons* than any sitcom in broadcast history."

Once your eyes are open to the theology in film and TV you will see it everywhere. Once you see it, what do you do about it?

USE FILM TO TRIGGER A CONVERSATION

Having seen the life questions and theology emerging in film, you can make these themes the basis for cultural conversations about the centrality of the gospel for all of life. Films provide a common language (pop culture) and a series of provocative themes as springboards for conversation or as illustrations showing the relevance of the gospel.

Chuck Colson tells of a conversation that was going nowhere with a prominent journalist . When he talked about his experience, the journalist countered with "That's great for you, but I don't believe in Jesus"; when Colson talked about eternal life, the journalist parried with "Death is final, there is no afterlife"; when Colson talked about the Bible the journalist retorted, "All legends."

But then Colson introduced Woody Allen's *Crimes and Misdemeanors* to illustrate the problem of human sin, the conscience, and guilt. In the movie, Judah Rosenthal kills his mistress and is overcome with guilt. Eventually the murder is pinned on a burglar. Judah breathes easier, and his guilt fades. By the end of the movie, we realize Judah has committed two murders; he killed both his mistress and his own conscience. Colson then asked the journalist, "Are you Judah Rosenthal?" The journalist laughed nervously. Colson reports that only when he used the contemporary metaphor of film did the "lights" go on and productive conversation ensue.

I interviewed Robert Duvall when he was nominated for an Oscar for *The Apostle*. He told the story of a deliveryman who stayed on the set to watch the filming of the preaching scene with all the gospel preachers. As Duvall tells it, "He came under the conviction of the Holy Ghost, dropped to his knees, and the evangelists saw to it that he got born again right on the set!" This inspired me to suggest to our listening audience that they invite a spiritually restless friend to see the movie and then go for coffee afterwards to discuss the film. Two weeks later a listener from Seattle called and told of a post-film, three-hour conversation resulting in a decision to follow Jesus by a friend he'd known for ten years, but had never been able to even talk to about Jesus. Informal, after-film conversations over coffee offer great opportunities to listen to your friend's views and share your own.

BECOME A FILMMAKER

For the long term, we should encourage talented, gifted, persevering disciples to learn the filmmaking craft. Their passion for the craft and giftedness should be the basis of their calling. Spielberg and Kubrick secured a platform for their worldview, not because of their ideological agenda, but because they mastered the technique and craft of filmmaking. They mastered the craft because they love it with a consuming passion. This mastery and devotion to craft is the working out of the image of a creative God through their unique gifts. In a sense, by virtue of the way God crafted them, they were born and destined to be storytellers in a visual medium and had the good fortune to be born in our technological age so wonderfully suited to their gifts. Ages ago, Spielberg and Kubrick would have been the guys drawing pictures on cave walls or acting out dramatic tales at the campfire. We need to identify young people gifted in visual storytelling and encourage them to pursue their passion.

Often, Christian discussions about entering Hollywood as professionals are mission driven more than gift driven. I hear exploitative, strategic, militaristic terms like "infiltrate" or "penetrate" Hollywood. Such an approach may enlist highly motivated young people, but mission without passion and giftedness will never produce the quality and authenticity necessary to produce truly influential work. A mission-driven person without talent is destined for Samuel Johnson's critique of a budding writer: "Your manuscript is both good and original, but the part that is good is not original and the part that is original is not good."

We do not need a bunch of young, aspiring, Christian filmmakers entering the profession as a vehicle for downloading their viewpoint. Such efforts inevitably produce shallow, jargonistic, and propagandist work. What we need are talented storytellers whose cinematic prowess earns them the right to tell the gospel story. In *Boundless Webzine*, Roberto Rivera, a fellow at the Wilberforce Forum, correctly observes, "Our culture has deemed the Christian story irrelevant. But, just as people need stories, they need something to believe in. And once you've decided that 'something' isn't in organized religion, specifically Christianity, then you'll take your experience where you can get it, and for many people, that's at the movies." For gospel stories to reenter American consciousness, we must take them to film, but they must be told well. That calls for the magical, exquisite blending of artistic integrity with a subtle, textured message conveyed naturally by believable characters in well-conceived plots.

For a filmmaker, writer, or producer to deliver a nuanced gospel, he or she must understand and embody it personally. This means we need to arm the next generation with a fully integrated, incarnational, inviting theology. Why do so many attempts at introducing a Christian worldview in film degenerate into dialogue full of simplistic jargon? It is because inadequately discipled Christians with a simplistic, jargonistic view of salvation and the gospel created them.

PRAY FOR FILMMAKERS

We should recognize that God loves the people who make films, and we should pray for them and for Christians with access to them.

Hollywood personalities are people God loves. Christianity has touched many of them along the way. In a 1997 *Out* magazine article, I read that Woody Harrelson "took solace in religion growing up, attended college on a scholarship from a Presbyterian church. 'You know, I was a Christian, I was active in church and had Bible studies at the house and stuff—youth group. I found that a lot of Christians were really cool. But there's definitely a percentage that are extremely judgmental and hypocritical and self-righteous.'" A 1999 *People* magazine article reports that Tom Hanks became a born-again Christian for a few years, joining the First Covenant Church of Oakland. Hanks said, "It was one of the best things I ever did. I had been a confused kid . . . religion helped me." Rene Russo has shared how C. S. Lewis's *Mere Christianity* has influenced her, Wes Craven attended Wheaton College, and Brad Pitt is a former *Young Life* leader who said recently in *Rolling Stone*, "You're talking to this guy who's always had this kind of congenital sadness. I know I'm the guy who has everything. But I'm telling you, once you get everything, then you're just left with yourself."

These people wield a disproportionate influence in society and especially on our kids. Instead of bemoaning their influence, we should recognize them as fellow humans on a spiritual journey and pray that they will be receptive to God as he reaches out to them. There are many Christians in Hollywood working side by side with these influencers. We should pray for them and the impact their lives and words can have on these cultural icons, who, by the way, happen to be people too!

And so film is not the always the enemy. It can be our ally. It allows us a window on the world to better see and understand people God loves. It facilitates dialogue about the centrality of the gospel for all of life. It provides what we need to tailor the gospel message for today's generation.

CHAPTER 19

■ Read the Books

A LITERARY FRIEND JUST CALLED TO report on a disturbing new book he is reading. "Depressing," he said, as he reflected on the author's successful foray into a previously unexamined area of his thought.

A good book is like that. It insinuates its way into our life and mind, flying low under our protective radar, leading us to places we would not voluntarily go. Vicariously experiencing alien places and coming out safe on the other side can equip us to understand the gospel and share it with other people. They too have been places we have never been, but when hearing their story we are reminded of what we have learned in the good books, that God and his gospel are there and are sufficient for every human story.

THE PUZZLE OF GOD

It was Sunday and we headed off to church, as is our usual custom. This, however, was our first Sunday back in Seattle, and we were prepared for the usual adjustments to life in a new church. As we pulled into the parking lot, I was intrigued, then pleased by the sight of a rather disheveled-looking man, head down, face unshaven, clothes wrinkled, ambling into the church. *Looks like the church demographic has diversified,* I thought to myself.

Since we were late, another usual custom of the Staubs, we slipped into a back row where I had a good view of the mystery man a few rows ahead and to the left. He had a way of tilting his head so that even when he looked up, he never made eye contact. I found my heart going out to him. Just before the sermon he got up to leave. I heard a silent voice say, "Go talk to him." I said, "Please, not today." The voice repeated the message, "Dick, get up and go out and talk to him."

I want to make it clear. I do not hear an audible voice when I get these promptings, but this little voice is real and I'm trying to recognize it, listen to it, and obey it. So I got up and caught up with the mystery man just as he was about to exit the building.

"Hi, I'm Dick Staub. Is everything okay?"

"Not really." He tilted his head sideways and in that indirect way glanced up at me and then immediately looked away.

"What brought you here today?" I asked.

"I want to know what God is going to do about Loraine," he shot back.

When I get in these situations, my mind travels a million miles a minute. I'm silently asking God to lead me to the right questions and optimal responses. Obviously the "what brought you here today" question provoked a visceral response, making me aware that I was in over my head and could only trust God to direct. There is a flow and dependence on the divine in these "God-thing" conversations that is both exhilarating and frightening at the same time.

"Who is Loraine?" I asked.

His voice dropped to an ominous whisper. "Two years ago tomorrow, my wife, daughter, and niece were all killed in an automobile accident when the car my wife was driving was hit head-on by Loraine. Loraine was drunk and driving on the wrong side of the street. It was her third drunk driving offense, and this time she killed my family. I want to know what God is going to do with Loraine." Thus began my first conversation with John. Emotional, intelligent, and intense, it lasted over an hour and began a process and ongoing dialogue that hopefully is bringing some healing to John's tormented soul.

Here is what is so eerie about that conversation with John. The next day I received a review copy from Warner Publishing. They wanted me to interview the author, Irish novelist Niall Williams, who burst onto the literary scene a few years earlier with *Four Letters of Love* and was now on tour with his new novel, *As It Is in Heaven.* I picked it up and started to read the opening lines.

> There are only three great puzzles in the world, the puzzle of love, the puzzle of death, and, between each of these and part of both of them, the puzzle of God. God is the greatest puzzle of all. When a car drives off the road and crashes into your life, you feel the puzzle of God.

The narrator interjects the question, "Whose fault was it?" And then tells the story of his wife and ten-year-old daughter killed in a head-on collision with a drunk priest. "Whose fault was it? My wife's, my daughter's, the priest's? Or was it mine." The narrator concludes it must be his because he is the one left on earth to grieve. This line of questioning is played out through the rest of the novel, a romance that blooms on a lattice of theological questions. The book helped me enter John's world in a way I couldn't have just a day earlier.

ENRICHING YOUR LIFE WITH BOOKS

Good books will enrich your life. Great writers, artists of all types possess two qualities—a clearly defined point of view regarding reality, and a unique signature style for communicating what they see. If you want to understand how your fellow humans struggle with contemporary life, read today's fiction.

In my experience good fiction often functions like the canary in the coal mine. It sees life as it is, gasps out observations to those who will hear, and gives us a chance to puzzle through our questions, layering and thickening them with the life experience of another. Without saying so directly, through the characters and the situations they face, fiction can urge us to take action or face certain doom.

All of our reading requires discernment. T. S. Eliot said, "It is necessary for Christian readers to scrutinize their reading, especially of works of imagination, with explicit ethical and theological standards." This is especially true with the explosion of "spirituality" books.

It would be hard to imagine a time when fiction and nonfiction have focused so openly on spiritual journeys. The bestseller list is packed with religious titles reflecting the widest range of theologies. The following is just a sampling of religious titles that made the *Publisher's Weekly* best-seller list: *Talking to Heaven, The Celestine Prophecy, Cloister Walk, Journey into Healing, The Bible Code, Embraced by the Light, Conversations with God, The Good Book, The Culture of Disbelief, Book of Virtues, Just As I Am, Left Behind, Chicken Soup for the Soul, Traveling*

Mercies, and more. Reviewers are watching this trend with great interest. A *Chicago Sun Times* critic described Salman Rushdie, author of *The Ground Beneath Her Feet,* as a writer "at play in the fields of rock, sex, and religion." The *New York Times* summarized John Updike's *The Lilies of the Field* as "seeking salvation on the silver screen." *Publishers Weekly* noted that while general trade book sales have increased 9 percent, the religion category has increased 13 percent in the years 1995–1998.

Behind each book is a fellow human, the author, wrestling with life's issues. Norman Mailer won the Pulitzer prize when he was twenty-five years old. Early on it was his ticket to free expression—unlike most writers, he could write whatever he wanted and still get it published. Eventually it became his tailor-fitted cross to bear, a weight of past glories and expectations beyond fulfillment.

By the time I caught up with him, he was a seventy-five-year-old man reflecting on this fact. "Fifty years ago I was an unknown writer, alone in a room with a blank sheet of paper and a pencil. Now today, I am still an unknown writer, sitting alone in a room, albeit a nicer room (in this case the Four Seasons in Chicago), with a blank piece of paper and a pencil."

I would have questioned his lack of notoriety had I not just struggled to explain to the twenty-eight-year-old at the hotel desk that I needed Norman Mailer's room, spelled M-A-I-L-E-R, not M-A-H-L-E-R as she had suggested. As I was packing up my tape recorder, after what he referred to as a "rugged hour" of conversation regarding *Time of Our Times,* he blurted out, "I wish I would have known you were a seminary grad, I would have gone out drinking with you. I used to get drunk and talk about women; now I get drunk and talk about God. I'm obsessed with God."

"Really, and what have you learned about God?"

With great intensity he raised his thick hands to gesture. "God is imminent. He's closer than I had ever imagined. It's as if I could reach out and touch him."

"And who is this imminent God?"

"I've concluded God cannot be both all-loving and all-powerful. If he was both he could not allow something like the Holocaust to happen. So, I've concluded he is all-loving but not all-powerful."

"And what about Jesus?"

"When I did my book on Jesus, I read the gospels very closely. Jesus was a true revolutionary with an inclusive message of love. Then along came Paul and organized religion, and they screwed the whole thing up with rules, bureaucracy, exclusivism, and judgmentalism. The very people Jesus accepted and hung out with, the church began to exclude." And so it went for another fifteen minutes, one of the twentieth century's most prolific writers reflecting on his wrestling with Jesus and God.

When your eyes are open to see, you realize theology is everywhere in contemporary fiction. Among Margaret Atwood's many literary feats is *The Handmaid's Tale*, a sobering story of a repressive, anti-woman, dictatorial government which derived its views from a rigid fundamentalist religious authoritarianism. I interviewed her on a later book and found her most provocative. I asked her what kind of feedback she received about *The Handmaid's Tale* from fundamentalist Christians. She replied with an impish grin, "None, nor would I expect any from a group that doesn't read serious fiction."

On the subject of her own religious sojourn she became more serious and animated. Her father was a scientist involved in field research, so she spent summers each year in the wilds of Canada, returning to civilization and school each fall. In Canada's public schools Scripture was read at the beginning of each day, and she developed an early interest in religion. Her parents did not discourage this pursuit, and by the time she was twelve, she was engaged in deep theological discussion with a local Presbyterian youth pastor about issues ranging from predestination to infant baptism. When she headed off to college, her fascination with issues of faith led her to enroll in the Bible-as-literature courses.

Reflecting on her own work, she bemoaned biblical illiteracy. "The Bible is Western civilization's essential document. You can't understand my writing unless you understand the basic underlying stories and themes of the Bible." Later, off the air, she told me some witty personal stories about her New Age mysticism and superstition, which I took as the restless experiments of a woman on a spiritual journey.

I was saddened by her portrayal of fundamentalist Christians as uninterested in serious fiction. For the most part I think she is probably right. Yet, though many did not read it, I remember hearing fundamentalists trash *The Handmaid's Tale,* dismissing it as an antireligious, pro-abortion tract. From my perspective, Margaret Atwood's point of view has been forged in the fires of her own experience and builds on a foundation of a rigorous contending with the Bible. Listening to her voice, and that of other writers, gives Christians an opportunity to see ourselves as many others do, to see how our beliefs appear when seen through a different lens and to frame a response based on our love and respect for a fellow sojourner on life's road.

In the past few years, publishers have released works of immense literary beauty and theological probing: *Mr Ive's Christmas* by Oscar Hijuelos, *Atticus* by Ron Hansen, and *Damascus Gate* by Robert Stone, to name a few. Some raise questions for which we need to frame a response. Consider the questions raised by a character in the Amy Bloom novel, *Love Invents Us.*

> Sometimes God makes a mistake. Just carelessness. He doesn't check the calendar. If He had checked, He might have seen that Elizabeth was overbooked for loss. Elizabeth didn't believe in a real God, but she had a God character in her head, part Mr. Klein, part

Santa. In grade school, when Mimi Tedeschi's little brother died, Mimi leaned forward from two seats back to whisper that God took him to be one of His angels. Elizabeth almost stood up in the middle of spelling to scream. Who could believe such ugly, cruel nonsense? That God would steal babies from their families because He was lonely, snuff the life out of them because He needed company?

The spiritual nature of today's fiction reflects the spiritual quest of contemporary writers, but it also reflects the appetites of a reading public, hungry for some satisfying spiritual reality. In May 1999, *Newsweek* reviewed best-selling authors Jan Karon, Anne Lamott, and Iyanla Vanzant and concluded, "By focusing on spiritual themes, three best-selling women authors have inspired huge and devoted followings." Most interesting was their report of Anne Lamott's observation that she "detects a great hunger in her liberal, literary audiences for spiritual fulfillment."

THE BENEFITS OF A GOOD BOOK

So how does a follower of Jesus benefit by taking the time to read a good book? Readers receive personal enrichment, an opportunity to understand another point of view, a chance to share time with an interesting person who has taken the time to put their viewpoint in writing, and the ability to wrestle through questions and frame responses. Public reading groups offer a chance to wade into a serious discussion of life issues and to interact with fellow sojourners, listening to their views and offering your faith perspective when appropriate. Instead of bemoaning the influence of Oprah's sometimes New Age book picks, why not exploit their popularity by reading them and discussing them from your Christian vantage point?

Good books offer opportunities for immense personal pleasure *and* effective engagement of your peers. The apostle Paul connected with the Athenians at Mars Hill because he knew the theological issues they wrestled with through their literature, which he obviously had read, saying, "For 'In him we live and move and have our being'; as even some of your own poets have said, 'For we too are his offspring'" (Acts 17:28).

As followers of Jesus our ability to influence people around us will be in direct proportion to our understanding of their issues and the gospel's response to them. Read good books. Enjoy and employ them for the kingdom.

CHAPTER 20

TELL SHORT STORIES

THEOLOGIAN KARL BARTH ONCE made a lengthy and complex presentation to a group of students. Weary of Barth's verbosity, one of the students took advantage of the question and answer period to ask this question. "Dr. Barth, could you summarize the gospel on a postcard?" Barth replied, "Yes, I can, young man—Jesus loves me this I know, for the Bible tells me so." The great theologian sat down.

What you know about the gospel should fill a book, what you

share about the gospel in any given situation may at times be reduced to a postcard. Jesus was a master of the short story, as you should be too. This means you should be able to present the gospel provocatively in bite sizes without oversimplifying it. The fact that Jesus did this in an age that was slower paced means we need to master this art even more effectively in this McAge.

A talk show host is an unlikely source for expertise on brevity. For over a decade, I spent three hours daily, every Monday through Friday from 4 P.M. to 7 P.M., hosting a radio talk show. Can you imagine fifteen hours a week of intense talking and listening and getting paid for it! After I'd been off the air for a few months, my sister observed my capacity for gab and said, "Dick, you need a radio show, because you have three hours worth of stuff to say each day, whether anybody wants to listen or not!"

I once spoke at devotions for Tyndale House Publishers, and I chose to speak on "words." I asked one of their marketing guys, Dan Balow, to calculate how many words they had placed on the printed page in the previous year. The total was 849 billion, 359 million words (and this was before the *Left Behind* series!). I point this out to say that neither publishers nor talk show hosts suffer from a shortage of words.

But in today's fast-paced world, communicators face a daunting challenge. We may have no shortage of words to say and write, but now people dedicate a decreasing amount of time to listening and reading. Jonathan Franzen, author of the critically acclaimed *The Twenty-Seventh City*, described his challenge as a novelist this way. "The novelist has more and more to say to readers who have less and less time to read: where to find the energy to engage a culture in crisis when the crisis consists in the impossibility of engaging the culture?" People today are busy and their time is fragmented. They need to hear what we have to say, but given the dynamics of contemporary life, we need to say it succinctly and quickly or they won't hear it!

Writers may be reassured by none other than William Strunk, author of the classic *Elements of Style,* who says, "Vigorous writing is concise. This requires not that the writer make all his sentences short, but that every word tell." I'm reminded of the rejection letter sent from a publisher to an aspiring young writer. The editor said, "I have every confidence that inside this very thick book is a thin one dying to get out!" Ask the whimsical wordsmith e. e. cummings if brevity means one cannot communicate effectively. His classics include the following lines: "Candy is dandy but liquor is quicker" and "When God decided to invent everything, he took one breath bigger than a circus tent, and everything began."

I bring good news for oral communicators who need a brevity makeover. It comes from none other than the master communicator, Jesus. More people have read and heard his teaching than any other teacher in history. Yet he was a man of relatively few words. His communication consisted of parables and simple stories with a moral lesson. He offered homespun stories drawn from universal tales or experiences common to his listeners. Everybody listening to Jesus could relate to his story about a wayward son or the story of a farmer who scattered seed, some of which failed to take root. Through these common tales, Jesus drew attention to spiritual issues in a nonconfrontational way but in a way that provoked response. Even in the Sermon on the Mount when Jesus spoke for an extended period of time, he still offered short nuggets built around the familiar—salt, light, treasure, neighbors, hypocrites, bosses, trees, clothes, food.

In addition to brevity, today's audiences crave stories. Josh McDowell's early communication style on college campuses was highly propositional. In debate-like fashion, he would make a logical and linear presentation of his case and would parry each counterargument made against him. This approach was captured in his book *Evidence Demands a Verdict*. In 1998 McDowell wrote fiction for the first time. When I asked him why he decided to try fiction, he said, "It has become obvious to me that the only way I can draw today's student in is to begin with stories that allow us to form a relational bond. Eventually I can get to propositional teaching, but not if I don't start with stories!"

It should be obvious that as a disciple you are trying to communicate the gospel in a world needing brevity and story. The good news is, Jesus, our discipler, shows us how to do it!

Jesus knew the elements of a good story. A good story is simple. It hooks us early. It builds on common experience, language, and symbols. It sets up a tension between characters, so people begin almost subconsciously making choices. It facilitates imagining. While it may contain many layers, it raises one key issue or makes one key point. Though the story is simple, the issue to be resolved may be complex.

Having engaged our heart, a good story lingers in our mind.

George Lucas has engaged an entire generation with his *Star Wars* story. Roberto Rivera, a fellow at the Wilberforce Forum at Prison Fellowship, sees these implications for communicators, saying in *Boundless Webzine*:

> If you want to engage people where they really live, you've got to reach for more than their heads or even their hearts. You've got to engage their imaginations. Once you've got that, chances are the rest will follow. In other words, if you want to teach a moral lesson, there is no substitute for a good story.

Tell Your Story

As Jesus' disciple, you should be able to tell at least one story— your own! People may be uninterested in your theology or knowledge of the Bible, but most people will be interested in your story. Your story should be built around the defining moments in your spiritual journey. Each of those defining moments becomes a nugget. Like Jesus, you should be prepared to share one nugget or to string together a series of nuggets like he did in the Sermon on the Mount. These nuggets may touch on different themes, and you will always want to choose the story that is most applicable to the situation you are discussing. You should be able to tell a story about why you decided to follow Jesus, about what it is like to follow Jesus, and why you continue to follow Jesus. You may want to tell a story about the hardest thing you've faced and how God or your Christian circle of friends helped you through it.

HEAR THEIR STORY

Hearing other people's stories is also important. I use a simple question to trigger dialogue. I simply ask, "Tell me a bit about your spiritual sojourn." The question is open-ended but focused enough to get the conversation going in a spiritually provocative direction. It is a reasonable question to ask if you've been talking about your spiritual experience or if your fellow conversationalist makes some observation about a religious theme in the news, music, or movies.

Triggering off film or pop culture is a great way to get conversations about spiritual journeys going, and the stories from popular culture can serve as a springboard for these discussions. For example, your friend sees an advertisement for the movie *Stigmata* and says, "What a joke!" You say, "Whoa, why do you think it's a joke?" Or Jesse Ventura says, "Organized religion is a crutch for weak people," and you ask your friend, "So what do you think about what Jesse Ventura said about religion?"

TAKE FIVE MINUTES

Ultimately your goal is to move naturally from your story or their story to the God and Jesus story. Knowing the essential

Bible stories is important because they will either provide a common starting point for discussion or allow you to initiate your fellow conversationalist into some of the greatest universal stories of all time. Even biblically illiterate people may remember the creation story, the story of the Fall, the story of Abraham offering Isaac, or the story of the Prodigal Son.

Today, most of our opportunities to tell stories come serendipitously while traveling on a plane, waiting in line, or sitting at a ballgame. This means we need to be available when the opportunity for discussion arises, which means we need to be prepared to modify our schedule to seize such a moment. For me, a type-A Swissman, such advice is very difficult to take. But I received some help a few years ago when I interviewed the author of a book called *The Five-Minute Minister*. The author was saying that instead of going crazy with our daily interruptions to our schedule, we should put a five-minute time limit on what appear to be interruptions. He insisted that by doing this I would discover some of my "interruptions" are actually divine appointments. His book came out around the same time as Richard Swensen's *Margins,* which states that we need to leave margins in our schedule, allowing more flexibility for the unexpected and taking some pressure off ourselves.

Being a time management freak, these were alien, loony ideas to me, but worth trying for the sake of the kingdom. I noticed that by setting a five-minute clock on interruptions, I relaxed because I knew I was only going to "lose" five minutes with the person interrupting my perfectly planned schedule. I also noticed that I could almost always satisfy the interrupting person by taking five minutes to hear them. And I noticed that often something important emerged out of these moments. I began to see that life is truly about what happens on the way to our destination, not the efficient and effective arrival at our destination. Sometimes the interruption is the day's purpose and is, in fact, our unscheduled destination.

I recently read an obituary for Dan Worral, a man I never met who obviously had a heart for people and had learned to live with margins. His wife of twenty-nine years said in his obituary, "A friend of ours said, 'Don was the slowest man I ever met but got more done than anyone I know.' Don had his own schedule. He took time to talk to a friend he chanced to meet or enjoy a beautiful day. He let the important take precedence over the urgent. I told Don, when you die, people won't think you're gone, they'll just think you're late again!"

Dan Worral was like Jesus that way. Ever notice how often Jesus' ministry happened while he was interrupted on his way to somewhere else? He would stop, listen, tell a brief, provocative story, and then he was on his way. Probably sometimes the whole thing took less than five minutes.

Hmmm. Brief stories. Think you have time to try it?

Be Humble

THOMAS MOORE SAID, "LORD, PLEASE help me always to seek for the truth, and spare me the company of those who have found it." The most unpleasant people I know are those who believe they exclusively know the truth and make the coercion of others their primary task. On the distribution curve of such obnoxious people, it often seems there is a disproportionate aggregation of religious types. Sadly, in addition to failing the test of intellectual rigor, they often manage also to fail the test of humility.

The problem has been complicated by the conflation of a Christian agenda with a political one. During the heat of political battle, when Clinton bashing was in full swing and Oliver North was running for Senate, a sign appeared at a Christian Coalition rally. It read, "Where is Lee Harvey Oswald when you need him?" The Coalition removed the offending sign and blamed the hostile poster on an extreme faction within its membership. But for many this sign symbolized the degree to which political activism has overwhelmed basic Christian decency and dignity in American political life. Many Christians have allowed political combat to replace making disciples and have allowed ideological confrontation to replace being a blessing or loving our neighbors.

The problem is not confined to political life. There is a growing and manifest distastefulness in the attitude of some Christians toward people disagreeing with them politically or ideologically. They possess an us-versus-them approach compounded by an unwillingness to listen and discourse about areas of disagreement. Today's argumentative society is more concerned with winning than in seeking truth and is therefore more comfortable demonizing opponents than respecting them. This phenomenon is not exclusive to Christians, but concerns me most among Christians, because such attitudes are inconsistent with following Jesus and inhibit our effectiveness when communicating Jesus' love to the world.

In a proud, strutting age, Jesus' disciples are called to a countercultural spirit and attitude of humility. Jesus himself was unceremoniously born in the equivalent of a barn. He grew up in small, insignificant towns. His father was a blue-collar carpenter. Though rabbi to a growing number of disciples, Jesus had no home. He taught that the meek and poor in spirit were blessed. He conveyed truth lovingly, showing flashes of anger only toward those within the religious community who lacked humility in the content and attitude of their teaching.

Facing crucifixion, though fully capable of claiming his rights and position as God's Son, he did not press his defense when brought before the high Priest and then Pilate. Instead, when he was asked by the High Priest if he was the Messiah, his reply was provocative but brief. When Pilate asked him if he was the King of the Jews, Jesus replied only, "You have said so." When taken to Herod, though questioned at some length, Jesus made no answer.

Jesus' behavior set a memorable example for his disciples. The apostle Peter admonished the earliest Christians to "clothe yourselves with humility in your dealings with one another, for 'God opposes the proud, but gives grace to the humble'" (1 Peter 5:5). The apostle Paul reminded the Philippians to clothe themselves with "compassion, kindness, humility, meekness, and patience" (Colossians 3:12).

This humility was not based on timidity of personality; one would be hard pressed to categorize Peter, Paul, or Jesus as diminutive, Milquetoast men. Nor was such a humility and meekness indicative of a weakness of ideological position or lack of intensity of belief. The Greek word for meekness, *praotes*, is commonly understood to mean self-control. As William Barclay says, the familiar Beatitude could have been translated, "Blessed is the man who has every instinct, every impulse, every passion under control." He also points out Aristotle's general definition of virtue as the "middle between two extremes," and specific definition of meekness as the "happy medium between too much and too little anger."

The pathway to such humility is through the mind. The apostle Paul urges the Romans, "[Do] not think of yourself more highly than you ought" (Romans 12:3). Humility begins by getting ourselves in proper perspective. We must "in humility regard others as better than ourselves. Let each of you look not only to your own interests, but to the interests of others" (Philippians 2:3–4). Nobody was superior to Jesus, so we can conclude that Paul is saying true humility means assuming a mindset of equality (which in Jesus' case, and perhaps yours, may not be true), then deferring to the other person in your conduct and attitude toward them. Were we to convey such an attitude in our life and witness in the world, what a difference it would make.

But how can we attain such an attitude, specifically when communicating our beliefs in daily life? Here's what I have learned.

I AM NOT GOD

Many Christians make the leap from "the Bible is God's Word" to "I am speaking for God" with relative, albeit misguided, ease. They then assume an authoritative position in every debate and a judgmental attitude toward every opponent. After all, "I am speaking for God."

In reality, even a genuine, bona-fide prophet like Isaiah acknowledged that God's thoughts were higher than his thoughts and God's ways higher than his ways. No human can claim an all-encompassing understanding of God, and no human can speak on behalf of God. The more an individual claims to speak for God, the less I trust them. I agree with writer Anne Lamott, who observed in *Bird by Bird,* "You can safely assume you've created God in your own image when it turns out that God hates all the same people you do."

I AM NOT JESUS

There were points in his ministry where Jesus issued judgmental and imprecatory condemnations. Usually these comments were reserved for religious types, like the scribes and the Pharisees—he made biting comments about the Pharisees being like whitewashed sepulchers. He condemned entire cities like Chorazin or Bethsaida for their disbelief. He cursed a fig tree for failing to produce fruit. He issued statements of woe against those who were stumbling blocks to children. He purged the temple of money-changers. In each case he was speaking in his unique role as a direct prophet of God.

Ours is not such a calling. In talk radio I've observed this assumption of prophetic mantle in some callers. There is this sense of solemnity and judgment. There is an assumption that they are speaking for God and that I will be cursed to eternal damnation if I don't fall at their feet and repent of my ways or views on a given subject. All this is based on their confidence that they speak with Jesus' authoritative, prophetic voice.

THE BIBLE IS LIMITED IN ITS PURPOSES

For many Christians the Bible has been reduced to their personal bludgeon, wielded to bring others to their position on virtually any subject about which they have gathered opinionated intensity.

Such people often begin with an assumption that the Bible is exhaustive in its revelation of all truth, at least in the subject matter to which they are devoted. Armed with this assumption, people have used the Bible to advance and defend very specific and detailed scientific, political, psychological, legal, educational, economic, philosophical, and apocalyptic theories.

On a more tactical, practical level, some Christians believe the Bible is a comprehensive blueprint for all personal behavior. Some use the Bible as a detailed parenting handbook, right down to admonitions for breastfeeding or the family bed. Others use it like a financial planning manual, including whether or not to take out a loan on a car or house, or what to do with your IRA or 401K, or whether or not to invest in gold or silver. The Bible was used as an advisory for proper planning for Y2K. It has been used to promote alternative medicine, homeopathy, chiropractics, and vitamin supplements.

In reality, while the Bible touches on and is useful for formulating life philosophies and prescribing daily behaviors, its overarching purpose is more narrowly defined. The Bible intends to draw humans into a restored relationship with God, with each other, and to the fulfillment of our original purposes as humans created in God's image. The Bible presents the drama of our creation, fall, and redemption and hints at our future as a human race. Even when we communicate within the purview of its purposes, we are to do so humbly. And we certainly should move with caution in seeking biblical affirmation for our specific philosophies and practices when they fall outside its purposes.

I SEE THROUGH A GLASS DARKLY

When you communicate from the Bible, you should be aware that what you offer is *your* understanding and interpretation of the Bible. The Bible is authoritative and adequately clear on the essentials of the gospel and principles for living, but there are numerous points at which the best I can offer is my "interpretation" of what the Bible teaches.

This led Augustine to advise Christians that we should, "in essentials require unity, in nonessentials allow diversity, in all things maintain charity." This requires that we discern between essentials and nonessentials and then properly interpret Scripture on the essentials. The church has a spotty record on exercising discernment. Until Copernicus came along in the sixteenth century, the church argued from Scripture that the universe rotated around the earth. Today there are those who argue from Scripture that the Caucasian race is superior to people of color. These examples illustrate that we may suffer from both an inability to discern what is essential and an inability to interpret the Scriptures properly. Most biblical literalists will acknowledge the errors in the examples I've cited, but are unwilling to acknowledge that they may be similarly mistaken in the contemporary issues around which they have gathered considerable passion.

Humility requires that we acknowledge that many of our beliefs and practices represent our personal understanding of Scripture, but are not binding on others. This means holding loose to a multitude of beliefs and allowing diversity within the broader culture and even within Christianity. This is very difficult for those whose confidence is based on being right in every case and who believe the Bible is absolutely clear in all things.

Christians who take comfort in bumper sticker platitudes like, "God said it, I believe it, and that settles it for me," rarely engage in dialogue with an ideological humility. After all, if what I believe is from God, and it differs from what you believe, "Duh—I win! God is on my side!" The glibness with which some Christians enlist God's authority in their quest to trump the ideological landscape is a reflection of the shallowness of their recognition of God's otherness and the limits this places on their comprehension of God and his revealed Word.

Bible teacher Harold Camping predicted the end of the world with complete certitude (although in the week before the predicted date he switched to 99 percent certitude). He based his prediction on detailed, intricate biblical interpretations and argued that the evidence was so compelling and clear that his was the only conclusion a reasonable person could reach. He was, we now know, mistaken.

I think of a *Wall Street Journal* cartoon in which a wife is saying to her husband, "Go ahead. Ask for directions. Think of it as getting in touch with your feminine side." My point? Many of us would rather cling to our misguided certitude than to admit that we lack certain details on the road of life.

I Have Not Arrived

There is often an immense gap between what I believe and aspire to and how I actually live my life each day. This in itself should produce a sizeable reserve of humility. Sadly, this is often not the case. In *Cloister Walk,* writer Kathleen Norris puts it this way, "My problem is that so many people who publicly identify themselves as Christians are such jerks about it. If being a Christian means incarnating the love of Christ in my own life, then maybe it would be best to let others tell me how well or badly I am doing." Our ultimate humility should derive from our awareness that Christianity is ultimately a life to be lived, not a set of doctrines to be believed. Our daily short-comings should remind us that we are more like unbelievers than unlike them. In this sense, we can honestly say, though we have found Jesus and follow him, we are still seekers and are fellow sojourners with all humans on the planet.

TRUTH WINS OUT

In the end, our humility and patience derive from our rock-solid belief that what we believe is true. In the event that our beliefs may be untrue, we welcome attempts to disprove our beliefs because we certainly do not wish to live delusional lives. I do not fear that my beliefs will be disproved, so I am not angry or insecure when attempts are made to do so.

Given the compelling support for what I believe to be true, I will press my case, but I will do so with all the humility God will grant (and some of my friends will say that God doesn't grant me enough!). I understand there are severe limits to anyone's ability to persuade another, and I understand that for most people a change of mind and heart comes as a result of a process, so I am satisfied to simply contribute my part to the process. This allows me to focus on influencing a person from point A to point B, instead of believing I can move them from point A to point Z. Understanding their skepticism, I embrace it rather than fear it. As John Stackhouse said in a Christianity Today article, "We try too hard to convince people that Christianity is true without first convincing them that it *might* be true."

So, the Christian who follows Jesus into the world should do so with humility because it is modeled by Jesus, commanded, and is the only proper approach given the fact that I am not God, that I see through a glass darkly, and that God is not finished with me yet.

CHAPTER 22

■ IN CONTROVERSY, SHOW YOU CARE

IF WE SPENT HALF AS MUCH TIME mastering the right spirit as we do mastering the right answers, our effectiveness in transforming culture would improve exponentially. Jesus called us to love. This does not mean we abandon our passion for truth or the use of our minds to reach logical conclusions. It does mean that we submit our truth-telling to the test of love. In debate, this means understanding the person as well as their ideological position.

After I interviewed feminist Susan Faludi about her new book

Stiffed, she shared some of her spiritual longings with me. I wondered if she had ever felt able to do so with her ideological combatants among Christian feminists. Would they rather defeat her ideas in debate or demonstrate God's love for her in relationship? Is it appropriate to win the ideological battle at the risk of losing a soul?

WHY DON'T YOU DO SOMETHING?

I remember a specific show in the early nineties on the subject of euthanasia. As usual on such a controversial subject, the phone lines were hot. Derek Humphries, founder of the Hemlock Society, was in the news, as was Dr. Kevorkian and his in-your-face attorney, Geoffrey Fieger. Ethicists and religious leaders were drawing lines in the sand and callers were full of opinions. I felt that too often Christians engaged such an issue with a black-and-white, drop-a-Bible-verse-like-a-grenade-and-run approach. While my convictions on the subject were clear and settled, my heart went out to people actually facing this tough decision with a comatose loved one. I wanted to nuance the discussion so we could hear and try to understand the person for whom this was reality and not a theoretical discussion.

"John in Edmonds, you're on the air."

"My wife died of cancer last year."

"I'm sorry to hear that, John. How does tonight's subject touch on that experience in your life?"

"My brother Paul is a Catholic priest. One night he and I were at the hospital to visit my wife, Carol. She was very brave. The last two years of her life she was in constant pain. It was hell. I wouldn't wish what she went through on my worse enemy, let alone Carol, who was the kindest, most giving, most loving person I've ever known, or ever will, for that matter." His voice choked. "I really miss her. It's still hard to talk about her."

"Take a deep breath, John. You're doing great. Thank you for helping us understand what you and Carol went through together. Can you tell us more about what happened?"

"Carol had asked me to help her die, and I didn't want to do it. Sometimes I felt like if I really loved her I would do this for her. All these doctors say they can control the pain. That's a pile of [expletive]. They'd drug her till she felt no pain and she'd be like a person in a coma. What kind of life is that? Then she'd cut back, but she'd be in gruesome pain, and that's when she'd want to die. She looked so small and helpless in that hospital bed, her eyes looked so far away when I'd leave at night. I never knew whether she'd be there when I came back the next morning."

"Anyway, this one night Jason, our sixteen-year-old son, stopped to visit Mom, and he started to argue with Paul. Jason had heard me talk with Paul about Carol's desire to end it all, and knew Paul was really holding the line. Paul's position was that no matter how right it might seem, it is always the wrong thing to do. Carol couldn't hear them talking. She was in a lot of pain that night. She skipped some medication because she wanted to be alert for Jason's visit."

"Then what happened?"

"Jason and Paul were kind of having this heated discussion when out of nowhere Carol began to scream out in pain. She started loud, then got quieter, then loud. It was this really scary combination of a moan mixed with screams, like somebody was torturing her. Then she started to call my name. 'John ... John ... I can't do this anymore. Please help me. I want to die. I can't take this anymore.'"

There are moments in radio, very few of them, when you feel you are in the middle of something so sacred and private, so deeply human, so visceral, so beyond the contesting of ideas and so rooted in essential and core human experiences, you feel like an intruder. You almost don't want to be there, but you are, and though totally wrapped up in the intensity of the moment, you try to figure out where this is going and what you're supposed to do. I didn't have to make that decision because John began to talk again.

"The rest of my life I'll never forget what happened next. Carol was screaming. Jason starting sobbing. Paul stood in the corner. He was really still, like he was frozen in place, out of place. The only light on was the lamp next to Carol's bed. I remember Paul looking very small and his silhouette on the wall was even smaller. Just then Jason turned and ran across the room towards me. He grabbed my shirt and pushed me up against the wall. His face was inches from mine. And he yelled, 'Why don't you do something, you [expletive]?'"

By now John's voice was quiet. I felt like he had spun a cocoon and we were all wrapped up in it. John didn't have a lot more to say. He talked about how he never did help Carol take her life. That Jason attended his mother's funeral but still wasn't speaking to Paul. That he felt ambivalent about his brother's spiritual counsel and advice. "It may have been right, but how can something so right be so wrong?"

The part of the call that has stayed with me to this day, is Jason's "why don't you do something, you [expletive]." It captured the depth of feeling in a person for whom this isn't an issue needing a right answer, but a person needing to express pain. Feelings don't change the ethical and moral conclusions on these issues, but people's feelings ought to affect the way we talk, teach, and preach about them. I always thought the phrase was a little too cute, "they don't care how much you know, until they know how much you care." Now when I think of John, I think of that phrase.

THE HUMANS BEHIND THE ISSUES

There is an interesting sidebar story to John's call. I was hosting a show on KING 1090 in Seattle at the time, but unbeknownst to me, was being monitored by the Salem Radio Network, a rapidly expanding network on the prowl for new talent. That night, Bob Ball, a seasoned veteran of Christian radio, monitored the show. Bob was a theologically conservative guy who had dealt with a lot of issues during his life and career, and had a lot of answers. But Bob had hit what was to be his final issue. Bob suffered from a terminal illness and was experiencing the slow but certain deterioration that would ultimately take his life. Not long before he died, Bob told me how much that broadcast meant to him personally. "It was a fine Christian treatment of a very difficult subject."

I found Bob's comment most interesting, because I never talked specifically about my religious beliefs that night. I asked him what he meant. Essentially he said, "That show was one of the few times I heard a Christian talk about the subject with an empathy for people experiencing the deep suffering I've known." Bob knew full well the value God places on life, and he had clear convictions on the issue of euthanasia. But Bob understood deeply and personally the "why don't you do something" aspect of this issue. And he knew that we would not be effective with the issues and answers until people knew we cared.

Behind every contested subject in the culture war are human beings like John, Carol, Paul, Jason, and Bob. Euthanasia. Abortion. Gay Rights. Fetal tissue research.

We can treat these subjects first as issues for which we have right answers, or we can treat them first as issues affecting people made in the image of God whom we love. What would Jesus do?

WAIT FOR GOD'S TIMING

THE LATE ORSON WELLS APPEARED in an advertisement in which he said, "We will serve no wine before its time." There are some things worth waiting for. The process of a spiritual journey towards God moves at its own pace. While you will often want to move your friends from A-Z in one conversation, the eternal God is satisfied with an incremental pace.

The apostle Paul recognized this progressive, step-at-a-time process when he likened spiritual development to gardening. "I planted, Apollos watered, but God gave the growth" (1 Corinthians 3:6). So the disciple does his part in the continuum of God's interventions with other people. And in his time, God does the rest.

JIM AND BOB

Here's a story to illustrate God's timing. They were two exceedingly unlikely candidates for the kingdom. Jim was a Viet Nam vet who by the age of sixteen had totaled his father's car, dropped out of high school, consumed considerable illegal beverages, and failed the tests of abstinence and safe sex. Then things got worse. He married his high school sweetheart and proceeded to continue his wild man ways, risking and losing their financial stake on more than one occasion, risking and nearly losing their marriage with numerous infidelities. His life in a shambles, he nevertheless was supremely confident and sublimely deluded into thinking that, given time and a few good breaks, he could turn this whole thing around.

Jim's brother, Bob, made Jim seem saintly. His parents sent him abroad during high school, hoping it would be an enriching, life-expanding experience. What they got instead was a son who discovered mind-altering exotic drugs, addiction, and the boorish, bohemian lifestyle of his newfound friends on the Continent. Back in the States, his brilliant technical aptitudes meant he could generate a substantial income while supporting his habit and living a Jekyll-Hyde, dual existence. He too felt under control until the ravenous appetites of his dark side began to increasingly intrude, uninvited and unmanageable, into his other life.

Of the two brothers, Jim was the first to awaken from his slumber. Having left his wife and children for the pursuit of freedom, fortune, and unfettered happiness, he soon realized he was not in control, but had inexplicably landed in a trough of pig slop of his own making. Not for the first time, but in fact for the last, he begged one more chance from his forbearing wife. This time there was a condition imposed on his return. Debbie had started attending a church called Willow Creek and found a relationship with Jesus. She insisted that if Jim wanted another chance, attending Willow Creek was the penance he would pay.

Bill Hybels, a pastor at Willow Creek, was preaching a series on the resolutions we make but never keep. Jim, needless to say, was something of an expert on this subject already. It had not occurred to him that the Bible would actually say anything remotely applicable to a contemporary human, so he was strangely discomforted by Hybel's words. Debbie was pleased and not mildly surprised when Jim actually made a favorable comment about the morning. "At least it's not a church." (Willow Creek is, of course, a church, but is always happy when someone like Jim is taken off guard by the experience.) It was months of Sundays and eventual participation in small groups before Jim's resistance turned to pursuit of Jesus. His spiritual journey commenced. Restored to his wife and family, the promise breaker became the promise keeper. And Jim began praying for his brother Bob.

Jim's desire for growth led him to Christian radio where, via the airwaves, he met folks like Alistair Begg, Dennis Rainey, and R. C. Sproul. His favorite shows were *A New Beginning* with Greg Laurie and the *Dick Staub Show* with yours truly. He liked Greg Laurie's humorous practicality, a combination appreciated by many of us as evidenced by Laurie's church being one of the ten largest in America. He discovered the *Dick Staub Show* when his wife recommended it to him. She liked it because she knew my wife. Eventually we met socially, and I heard Jim's amazing conversion story. Jim was particularly burdened for his brother Bob, and asked me if I would pray for him. Jim told me Bob was having some real problems. He had replaced his drug addiction with workaholism, and it was creating a strain on his marriage. I put him on a prayer list I keep in my Day-Timer and began to pray for him regularly.

On one occasion I met Bob, his wife, and son. I took a particular liking to Bob's ten-year-old son because conversation with him meant I didn't have to socialize with the adults at the party we were attending. Unbeknownst to me, this chance encounter with Bob and my friendliness with his son gained me two new listeners. This proved to be of eternal consequence for that family, ironically through the Greg Laurie connection.

Greg was scheduled to speak on a Tuesday night at 7 P.M. and agreed to stop by our studios for a 5 P.M. live interview. We were talking about Greg's personal conversion story and the conversion of his father. When a child, Greg was abandoned by his father and came to know him only later in life. Most remarkably, Greg's reunion with his dad included a spiritual discussion leading to his father seeking to be restored, not only with Greg, but with God as well. His father died not long after that. Greg's experience with his dad was an example of God's timing.

I remember feeling a bit overwhelmed with the realization that there were specific people listening at that moment for whom this story might trigger an openness to the gospel. I asked Greg a simple question. What advice do you have for the person, listening right now, who has not yet made peace with God like your father did?

Greg responded, "Remember when you were a kid? What would your mom say when you went outside to play? She'd say, 'Get home before dark.' My advice to anybody who hasn't made things right with God is to get home before dark. You don't know when you will die. Don't stay out too late. Come home now before it gets dark."

As soon as the interview was finished we hurried off to Greg's speaking engagement. There were over three thousand people in attendance and a real sense of expectation in the crowd. After I introduced Greg, I sat back and listened to one of Greg's classic, culturally relevant presentations of the good news of God's love. Greg ended his message with an invitation for those who wanted to make a commitment to Jesus Christ to come on down to the front. In a matter of moments the entire front of the sanctuary was filled with seekers. Praying quietly, I was surveying the group of over seven hundred when my eye caught a familiar face. First, I saw Bob's ten-year-old son. Then I noticed he was holding his mom's hand. And then, next to Mom, I spotted Bob. That night the whole family made decisions for Christ!

They were whisked off to a prayer room for counseling so it wasn't until the next day I heard the rest of the story. I learned that after the party Bob had decided I was an okay guy. His ten-year-old son was particularly impressed that there was a grown-up who thought like a ten-year-old (a quality my wife doesn't always find quite so endearing!). As a result, they both became listeners to the *Dick Staub Show*. Bob had also discovered *A New Beginning* in his morning drive. On Tuesday night Bob and family were driving to a PTA meeting with the radio on in the background. They heard Greg Laurie's story about his father. They heard my question about advice for those who had not yet made peace with God. They heard Greg's answer about getting home before dark. They also heard me mention where Greg would be speaking at 7 P.M. and realized it wasn't that far from their planned destination.

There are decisions we make without truly understanding their consequences. Jim's wife met mine and invited us over for dinner. Jim asked me to pray for Bob. We all decided to go to the party where I met Bob and his son. Greg made the decision to come on the *Dick Staub Show* even though he had a speaking engagement just two hours later. I made the decision to ask the "advice for the seeker" question. Greg decided to talk about getting home before dark. Bob decided in a split second to skip the PTA meeting to hear Greg in person. And then, in the most excellent decision of all, Bob and his family made the decision to "get home before dark" by receiving Christ.

We all know the phrase "timing is everything." In Ecclesiastes we are told "for everything there is a season and a time for every matter under heaven." Is there a "Bob" you've been praying for? Let me encourage you to pray, share your faith, and trust God for the timing. But if you are a "Bob" and you haven't made your peace with God, my advice for you is this: "Get home before dark!"

Expect Magnificent Defeats

"Of the making of many books there is no end, and much study is a weariness of flesh." So said the wise writer of Ecclesiastes. I am reminded of Walter Bagehot who said, "The reason why so few good books are written is that so few people who can write know anything." We have finally arrived at a chapter I am fully qualified to write. Please don't be deceived into thinking that this fine publisher set out on a national search to find the most successful and compelling Christian presence in the world to write about following Jesus, and that such a search landed them squarely at my front door. To the contrary, though I follow Jesus into the world each day, I am confident my failures far outweigh my successes. When it comes to failure I know what I'm talking about.

It was the first leg of my long journey from Chicago to Hong Kong by way of San Francisco. My travel aims were of the noble sort, for I was on my way to smuggle Bibles into China so the lost could hear the gospel. I, of course, would then come home to report their need and parenthetically to receive considerable adulation for my admirable sacrifice and risk-taking. However, I am sorry to say, I was evidently suffering from the spiritual myopia experienced by many who earnestly desire to save the whole world. For I was clearly not quite so keen in my compassion for the gay man sitting right next to me on the flight, because while usually gregarious, today I felt like being left alone. My mental calculations went something like this. He is gay. I am a talk show host on a Christian radio network. He probably despises Christian broadcasters because of a generally unloving, hostile attitude toward gays so often encountered there. Though he and I both detest these hostile words and attitudes, I am really, really tired and I just lack the energy to gain his trust and show him a different kind of Christian by working through all the obstacles I know will be there. Even though I felt a clear prompting to talk to this guy, I ignored that little voice, deciding it was a situation tailor made for disaster. In my weariness, I wanted no part of it.

So I began the solitary flyer routine. Frequent flyers know the moves. You inanely focus intently on a book or magazine, gazing vacantly straight ahead, never looking to the left or right. Your demeanor becomes that of Albert Einstein; you are processing deep and important thoughts that might shape the intellectual course of the human race. In times like these, when sitting next to such a brilliant intellect, any passenger in his right mind knows you do not disturb. Soon it became apparent all my diversions were unnecessary because, to my great relief, he too seemed uninterested in conversation. He was courteous and polite, but not the least bit engaging.

However, a few minutes before landing, I decided I was now ready to chat and asked him if San Francisco was home. "Yes," he replied. Then, "I'm returning from my mother's funeral in Iowa. She died of cancer. It really has me shook up." I now recognized the marks of human grief: a quiet reticence, a faraway look, an aching intonation and weariness in the voice, an uneaten meal, heavy sighs, a fitfulness when he tried to sleep. And the almost undetectable tears that had just now appeared at the merest hint of human kindness.

I was ashamed and rightfully so. The flight was ending. A fleeting and timely opportunity gone, I said I was sorry for his loss, and having secured his name told him I would pray for him for the next thirty days. He seemed genuinely appreciative. I described Nick Taylor's book *A Necessary End* and recommended he read it. Then we picked up our carry-on items and made our way into the crowded terminal where we went our separate ways, never to see each other again.

ANOTHER FAILURE

I want you to understand that I am a man of magnificent failures and defeats. My shortcomings are not reserved exclusively for strangers. I spread them around generously even to good neighborhood friends. For example, allow me tell you about Rob.

"So to whom does the Immaculate Conception refer?" Saturday night was the continuation of an ongoing conversation with Rob. Rob is an extremely successful consultant with a big heart and an unwavering commitment to personal integrity. He's the kind of guy who gets mad when he sees a consultant pad a client's bill or inflate an expense report to his own company. Honest, hard working, and immensely likeable, Rob is also openly restless and a seeker. I learned this last summer at Rob's surprise fortieth birthday party. Kathy and I were pleased we were invited, because while we always enjoyed this couple, we seldom saw them except at our kids' soccer games.

The party began with an open bar at a popular restaurant. By the time the guests sat down for dinner, the volume had grown loud and the speech of many was considerably slurred. Rob grabbed me and insisted I sit across from him, which again, given the limited nature of our previous relationship, was a surprising honor. "See this woman next to me?" he said, pointing to his wife. "She is a real Christian, a saint." He paused, and while she covered her face in embarrassment, he continued. "I, on the other hand, just can't seem to get it. I tell other people why they should believe in God, but I just can't seem to feel I am fully there myself."

By now the buffet was prepared and we were being summoned to corral our food. Another of Rob's friends sitting nearby leaned over and urged Rob to change the subject. "This is getting too heavy," she said. "Let's get something to eat!"

Rob urged the others to go ahead but waved at me to follow him. We ended up in a corner of the restaurant where he pumped me with questions. I tried to answer those questions and point him to Jesus. Being held hostage by the birthday boy in private, earnest conversation while his guests banqueted elsewhere was beginning to feel slightly rude, even to a socially obtuse creature like me, and I felt the need to deliver him back to his madding crowd.

So I suggested we finish our conversation another time and advised him to read the gospel of John. "I don't like to read, haven't read a book in twenty years," he responded. We worked our way back to the table where we changed the subject and a good time was had by all. But I wondered, had I handled this right? Should I have said or done something different?

The next week in talking to friends I repeated this story to illustrate the spiritual hunger that is all around us. I fully intended to follow up with Rob, but things got busy, he traveled, soccer season was over, and now a full year later we are sitting at his dining room table and I am being asked about the Immaculate Conception.

The answer, of course, is that the Roman Catholic doctrine of the Immaculate Conception refers to Mary. Rob was reporting that I was the first person he'd asked who didn't think it referred to the conception of Jesus. From this doctrinal perch we moved on to his report of a conversation he had with a very religious and learned woman who was reading a book claiming that Jesus sinned like the rest of us. The book included accounts of a spiteful and youthful Jesus using supernatural powers to get even with other kids who picked on him—kind of a supernatural Eddie Haskell. I was able to parry these myths from the apocryphal gospels and attempted to steer the ship back onto a more fruitful discussion of Jesus, but then the next guests arrived and Rob sprang his Immaculate Conception story on these Catholic guests. To Rob's delight they gave the wrong answer, and the opportunity for conversation was lost for the evening and perhaps forever.

I comfort myself with the knowledge that there is usually a progression of events and conversations in any person's conversion, but I feel that I let Rob down in failing to follow up on the birthday conversation. There was a wide open door, and I allowed my busyness to crowd it out.

THE WORLD AND MY NEXT-DOOR NEIGHBORS

My life with Jesus in the world is a succession of such failures and makes it difficult for me to try to urge others to follow Jesus into the world with a sense of personal integrity. Who am I to urge you to follow the "too-Christian, too-pagan route," when my own life is littered with stories of missed opportunities?

In the eighties I was very involved in challenging Christian professionals to accept international jobs so they could gain access to people needing the gospel but living in countries where missionary visas were not granted. At the time about 82 percent of the world's unreached people lived in countries inaccessible to traditional missionaries. So while over sixty thousand American missionaries worked abroad, most of them could not enter these restricted access countries. Meanwhile, over three million Americans lived and worked abroad, many of them in these restrictive countries. To me, the strategic implications were clear. We needed to help dedicated Christians get these jobs in closed countries and through them reach the unreached. It was exciting work and somewhat exotic given the opportunities for international travel. One of my friends, aware of my travel itineraries, believes to this day that I was on some secret mission for the CIA. Bulgaria, Romania, the USSR, China, the Middle East—my trips took me to unusual destinations and I was gone for weeks at a time.

Once, returning at 2 A.M. from one of these long, grueling trips, I saw an ambulance across from our house. Ed's wife, Stella, had just suffered a heart attack and was being taken to the hospital for emergency care. I realized that in all of my travels to save the world, I had abandoned my own neighbors. Another neighbor, Barry, had recently suffered the loss of his teenage daughter, murdered by the Green River killer, a serial murderer responsible for a string of homicides in one of America's most terrifying unsolved mysteries.

I'm more than aware of my neighborly failings. Next week we will be moving from this neighborhood where we have lived for eight years. In those eight years I have continued to influence others to be a faithful presence for Christ in their circle of influence, but I have again failed two neighbors right here.

Jan, our neighbor to the south, is a single mother of two boys who divorced her husband about three years ago. I'm friendly and cheerful enough, but I must confess, I've not gone out of my way to discover ways to help her and her sons through what has undoubtedly been a tough adjustment. At one time she talked of moving a caboose onto the back of her lot for her boy's enjoyment, and I along with other neighbors registered our strong concerns. In retrospect, I realize I've been more concerned that she keep her yard looking good to keep property values up, than I have been in finding out who she is and demonstrating Christ's love in practical ways. Fortunately, Ray and Debbie, Christians across the street, have been diligent in befriending Jan and showing her acts of kindness. Feels like they should be writing this book, not me.

Then there is my neighbor across the street. He moved into the neighborhood with his wife and teenage daughter a year ago August with the express purpose of getting their daughter out of a bad inner-city neighborhood situation. He works for the labor union and sports Hoffa bumper stickers to prove it, while the rest of the neighborhood is white-collar Republican. Last year, on the night before school started, he came over with his daughter to ask about the school bus schedule. We chatted and he seemed eager to please and be accepted.

A few weeks later Kathy hosted a back-to-school tea for the ladies on the block, and the new neighbor's wife showed up with her own coffee, which some of the other guests later insisted was spiked with vodka. Since that time her erratic behavior has left few neighbors doubting that behind those closed curtains is a troubled woman. Just before we moved out of the neighborhood, in the early morning as I left the house to walk the dog, my neighbor was watering his lawn. I said hi, our eyes met, and I saw a sad, heavily burdened man. This is just the kind of situation Jesus loved to enter, bringing restoration to individuals. But we're moving away. Another missed opportunity.

Why am I telling you these stories? Because with all the thrills of occasional victories for Jesus in the world, I, just like you, have had more than my share of magnificent defeats. What do I do with the knowledge of my regular failures?

I ask God to forgive me. I pray that God will consistently open my eyes to the people around me and make me receptive to his prompting. I try to learn from missed opportunities, and I try not to miss any new opportunity that comes my way.

I close with an admonition from Wes King, who puts it this way in his album *Room Full of Stories*.

Break my heart, open my eyes, fill me with compassion.
Show me how to be Jesus to the universe,
Jesus to the universe next door to me.

CHAPTER 25

BURN THE BOATS

FREDERICK BUECHNER SAYS IN *TELL-ing the Truth,* "The gospels disdain equally saccharine endings and soft-boiled hope. Rather they record the tragedy of human failure, the comedy of being loved overwhelmingly by God despite that failure, and the fairy tale of transformation through that love."

I've encouraged you to decide to follow Jesus into the world. I've urged you to experience the gospel, living it out and articulating it in compelling ways. Now I am asking you to endure to the end. Endure like my grandfather did.

My grandfather died in his seventies having served God all his life. The night before he died he watched the news and there was a report about a fast-growing cult. Grandpa went to bed. My dad had a cot set up in the room so he could help Grandpa in the night. In the middle of the night Grandpa awakened and asked Dad what could be done about this cult. A few hours later he died having uttered his last words, loving the lost until the very end.

Grandpa's favorite hymn was by A. B. Simpson, and he always urged me to make it mine.

> Lord, you have given me a trust,
> A high and holy dispensation,
> To tell the world, and tell I must
> The story of your great salvation.
> You might have sent from heaven above
> Angelic hosts to tell the story
> But in your condescending love
> On man you have conferred the glory
> We all are debtors to our race;
> God holds us bound to one another
> The gifts and blessings of his grace
> Were given us to give our brother
> We owe to every child of sin
> One chance, at least, for hope of heaven;
> Oh, by the love that brought us in,
> Let help and hope to them be given.
> Let me be faithful to my trust,
> Telling the world the story;
> Press on my heart the woe;
> Put in my feet the go;
> Let me be faithful to my trust
> And use me for your glory.

Beneath that archaic language beats the heart of a man who felt Jesus' compassion for the world and dedicated his